UNFOLDING BEAUTY · THE ART OF THE FAN

A Boÿse inct: prinihes: ,FÿIII:

UNFOLDING BEAUTY · THE ART OF THE FAN

Anna Gray Bennett

The Collection of Esther Oldham and the Museum of Fine Arts, Boston

THAMES AND HUDSON

First published in the United States in 1988
by Thames and Hudson Inc., 500 Fifth Avenue,
New York, New York 10110

First published in Great Britain in 1988
by Thames and Hudson Ltd, London

Library of Congress Catalogue
Card No. 86-63853

This book is published in conjunction with the exhibition
"Unfolding Beauty: The Art of the Fan,"
Museum of Fine Arts, Boston, Massachusetts
March 9 - June 5, 1988.

Printed in U.S.A. by Acme Printing Co.,
Wilmington, Massachusetts

Bound by Acme Bookbinding Co.,
Charlestown, Massachusetts

Designed by Carl Zahn

Text edited by Janet G. Silver

Frontispiece:
The Birth of Adonis (unmounted fan leaf). 1637-38
Abraham Bosse, France, 1602-1676
Engraving with etching, 1976.568

CONTENTS

· ·

PREFACE

The collections of the Department of Textiles and Costumes in the Museum of Fine Arts, Boston represent a diversity and quality rarely equaled. The fans brought to public attention through this book and exhibition reveal only one small facet of the department's rich holdings, of which the fan collection is generally considered to be the most extensive in North America. This publication offers a selection in full color of one hundred outstanding works produced in Europe and the Americas from the sixteenth to the twentieth centuries. Not included here are examples of our one hundred fans and fan leaves produced in the Far East.

The core of the collection of Western fans – 424 in all – came to the Museum in 1976 through Esther Oldham's generous gift of her famous treasures. An important earlier contribution was made by Elizabeth Day McCormick of Chicago in 1943. She donated to the Museum her great collection of several thousand works of art, including many exquisite fans. The Museum's fan collection began, however, much earlier; the textiles department archives document frequent bequests in the 1880s and 1890s from prominent Boston ladies who left their favorite fans to the Museum. At that time, a fan was still a refined costume accessory and not simply a curiosity to be collected. Several lovely examples included here came to us through these early bequests.

The idea for a book based on the Museum of Fine Arts fan collection emerged with Esther Oldham's magnificent 1976 gift. The project was realized through a grant from the National Endowment for the Arts, to which we are most grateful. The work of studying and selecting the objects, writing the book, and supervising the photography, was accomplished with distinction by our friend and colleague Anna Gray Bennett, former Curator of Textiles at the Fine Arts Museums of San Francisco. It is to her great credit that this long undertaking has been brought to such a fine conclusion. Deborah Kraak, Assistant Curator of Textiles and Costumes, and Karin Bengtson, Curatorial Assistant, were responsible for overseeing the departmental participation in this project. Their dedication and research, proofreading, and organizational skills are greatly appreciated.

It is our sincere hope that by introducing these fans to the public many may share our enthusiasm for Boston's outstanding ensemble of original and elegant "air conditioners."

JEAN-MICHEL TUCHSCHERER
Curator, Department of Textiles and Costumes
Museum of Fine Arts, Boston

ALAN SHESTACK
Director
Museum of Fine Arts, Boston

ACKNOWLEDGMENTS

My first thanks go to Jean-Michel Tuchscherer, Curator in the Textiles and Costumes Department at the Museum of Fine Arts, Boston, for the privilege of working with him and with this extraordinary collection. The mixture of media involved in fan manufacture meant many calls for in-house help from many different museum departments. I thank Philip Conisbee and Laurence Kanter of the Paintings Department; Jeffrey Munger and Sam Quigley, European Decorative Arts; Roy Perkinson and Eleanor Sayre, Department of Prints, Drawings, and Photographs; Wu Tung, Asiatic Art; and John Herrmann and Florence Wolsky, Classical Art.

Hélène Alexander, Nancy Armstrong, and Avril Hart sent information from England, Milton Sonday and Alice Zrebiec from New York, and David Hamilton from the West Coast.

The late Mrs. Henry W. Borntraeger, Esther Oldham's sister, and her niece, Mrs. John Logan Orser, furnished invaluable assistance in the form of biographical details and photographs. The catalogue project made demands on all members of the Textiles Department and all responded cheerfully and generously. I thank Deborah Kraak and Karin Bengtson for their meticulous review of the text and organizational assistance. Special thanks go also to the volunteers in the Department of Textiles and Costumes including Mary Lou Touart, for whom no task was too large or too small, and to Nancy Hollomon, Deborah McMillan, and Doris May.

A remarkable large-scale fan conservation effort was carried out by Margaret Leveque, Jerri Newman, Leslie Smith, and Leslie Ransick, and the volunteers under their direction, Ralph Bennett and Carol Warner. Over a period of several months, the fans were strengthened and their beauty was renewed. Gary Ruuska's photographs have captured that beauty with special brilliance.

A.G.B.

A SPLENDID OBSESSION, ESTHER OLDHAM, 1900–1984

Esther Oldham was born on January 11, 1900, in Welles-ley, Massachusetts, where she lived all but one of her eighty-four years. She and her sister, Anne, grew up in comfort and security in a day when houses were as yet unnumbered and townspeople called each other by name. Esther's parents provided a congenial family atmosphere, always encouraging individual talents and preferences. Each member played a musical instrument, had a favorite color, and pursued a chosen hobby. Esther played the violin, accompanied by Anne at the piano. At an early age each girl was given a gift of an heirloom: Anne a pewter teapot and Esther her great-great-grandmother's fan, which was framed and hung on her bedroom wall. At the age of ten, Esther's course as a collector was set. In 1984, looking back on sixty years of collecting, Miss Oldham said, "From that day onward, I vowed I would make a great collection and give it to the museum. Some nerve, wasn't it! But it came about, as you know."

As a teenager, Esther made fans her emblem, wearing fan pins on her dresses and carrying fans to dancing school. One time she chose a feather fan that proved deciduous, and the boys spent more time gathering up peacock eyes than dancing. While still in high school, Esther began to buy fans, rather haphazardly, because she loved them all. Palm leaf fans, souvenir fans, modern ones – she wanted "one of each," although she preferred eighteenth-century examples. Fans of that period were undervalued, but price was not the index. Miss Oldham recognized quality, and this, with diversification, was her guiding principle.

Meanwhile, her other pursuits were far from narrow. She played first violin in the Dana Hall orchestra and studied sculpture and lace-making, both of which illuminated certain technical aspects of fan-making. For more information about fans, she read the compendious volumes of George Woolliscroft Rhead and Lady Charlotte Schreiber. But the literature was otherwise meager, and so she researched the subject on her own, spending long hours in the Rare Books Room of the Boston Public Library. Before long, she was publishing articles on her specialty in such magazines as *The Connoisseur* and *Antiques*. In more than forty articles she gave a growing interest group information regarding fine points of fans and fan collecting. Perhaps her greatest contribution resulted from her investigation of the American fan factories operating in Massachusetts in the nineteenth century, which appear in *The Antiques Journal* (August and September 1953) and *Spinning Wheel* (January-February and March 1972). Shortly after World War II, Esther Oldham and a group of close friends organized the Fan Guild of Boston. They met a few times a year to exchange information and to socialize. The guild existed from about 1946 to 1961, when its members published *Fan Leaves*.

Along with literary activities, Esther Oldham continued to collect. Rarely attending auctions, she relied on favorite dealers to seek her out with pieces of particular interest. Her collection went far beyond the conventional limits of the period. It is tempting to think that the time she spent in Hawaii with her sister and brother-in-law, Colonel Henry Borntraeger, from 1930 to 1932 may have height-

Esther Oldham, 1945. *Photograph by Chalue.*

ened her appreciation of the art of other cultures and led her to collect ethnic fans from such distant places as Samoa, Indonesia, and Africa.

In the early fifties, Miss Oldham made her most important acquisitions from the famous collection of DeWitt Clinton Cohen. In 1976, when her collection had grown to over a thousand fans, she offered it to the Museum of Fine Arts in Boston, which accepted more than four hundred. Others went to the Peabody Museum in Salem, the Braintree Historical Society, and Old Sturbridge Village. Honors came from all directions, including a citation from the governor and a plaque from the Fan Circle International of London, of which she was a patron.

Esther Oldham belonged to that rare group of collectors whose single-minded pursuit of their art is matched by a desire to share it with others. Great museum collections throughout the world have been formed by this meeting of mind and heart, which transforms a private passion into a public treasure.

1. This biographical sketch is based on an interview with Miss Oldham's sister, the late Anne Oldham Borntraeger, in March 1986, and on a recorded interview with Esther Oldham herself conducted by members of the North American Fan Association in October 1984.

In the long centuries preceding technology, when we were richer in craft and poorer in comfort, decorative hand-held fans brought relief to an overdressed, overheated society. Shapes and materials varied according to taste, availability, and the culture that produced them. In the East, the arc of the fan leaf presented a challenge to the best artists, and fan painting became a recognized and respected art form. The sticks that supported the leaf remained elegantly simple, never detracting from its subtleties. In contrast, the sticks of Western fans vied with the leaves for attention, producing effects of novelty and brilliance. At their apogee, in the eighteenth century, Western fans were used indoors and out, summer and winter. As they became ubiquitous, they assumed a gamut of new functions. They were used, on occasion, as memory aids, for parlor games, or for political propaganda, as masks, lorgnettes, cryptic communicators, and, of course, accessories in the oldest game, when dalliance was a major preoccupation. They reflected the goals and values of those who carried them, and in use they revealed a temperament in motion.

The fan's rise to prominence began late in the sixteenth century, when fashion-conscious Henri III of France (r. 1547-59) introduced it at court, probably less as a cooling device than as an exquisite and novel accessory. The earliest fan in the Oldham collection (cat. no. 53) dates from the same period and is probably similar to the fan the king carried. It was made of skin cut out with a knife to resemble reticella lace. It was quite unlike its "feather duster" predecessor, familiar from early portraits of Elizabeth I. It complemented the costume in vogue, white against the usual Spanish black, crisp like the ruffs that set off the heavy, formal fabrics. (The stiffness of the ruffs resulted from the use of starch, recently invented in the French lowlands. The king is said to have personally supervised the starching of his lace.) The fan's novel feature was its ability to open and close "at a touch," thereby providing that essential element of fashion – surprise.

Fans had come to France from Italy with Henri's mother, Catherine de Medici, who also brought lace and perfume. Many local varieties had developed there, including the flag fan in Venice and the so-called duck's foot fan in Ferrara. The latter opened only to a quarter circle, but its ridges anticipated the pleats and supporting ribs of later versions. The route by which the folding fan had reached Italy is conjectural. Certainly, the rigid hand-held fans seen on Greek vases had disappeared centuries before, leaving only the great long-handled flabella to be waved by attendants protecting the host during the mass. The fan may have been reintroduced to Europe in the twelfth and thirteenth centuries by crusaders homeward bound with booty from the Middle East.

Once established at the Valois court, folding fans spread northward like a well-planned invasion. Those traveling by land met others brought in from the East by Portuguese and Dutch merchant seamen. These gradually took the place of the grandiose feather fans. Not only were the new fans more convenient, but it was perceived that they, too, could serve the cause of grandeur by offering a picture plane on which to display heroic deeds in miniature. A general change in mood hastened full acceptance. The rigid dress code, established in the sixteenth century under Spanish influence, relaxed. Ruffs drooped into falling collars, over which the luxuriant locks of cavaliers tumbled in planned confusion. The flourishes, the extravagance of manners and dress, reappeared in flamboyant fan borders framing the deeds of gods and heroes, as in Abraham Bosse's *Birth of Adonis*, designed for a fan leaf (frontispiece, 1976.568). His better-known engraving of a gallery in the Palais-Royal shows fans for sale with laces, gloves, and ribbons, examined by a group of exquisitely fashionable men and women as the shopkeeper reaches up for a box labeled "Fans by A. Bosse."

The opening of a sea route to the East by Vasco da Gama in 1498 and the success of the first merchant seamen resulted in the establishment of the great East India companies (English in 1600 and Dutch in 1602). The import business soon escalated to a grand-scale operation. Porcelain was the import in greatest demand. It seemed an almost magical substance, its composition and manufacture still a mystery in Europe, and it enriched those at both ends of the long voyage from Canton. Fans, considered less valuable as imports, were nevertheless included in the shipments, partly because of their transportability. Their decoration was often inspired by the porcelain they accompanied (see cat. no. 22).

The first imports may have truly reflected Chinese taste, but because there was profit to be made, the product was soon modified to please the consumer. Before long, fans represented an Oriental view of European taste. They were accepted uncritically, and even the tremendous volume exported was inadequate to meet the demand. The result was the manufacture in Europe of fans in the "Oriental" style, which, in turn, influenced those made in China and Japan for export. By this time, fans, in general use in European courts, reflected an infatuation with the Orient that continued to grow as the century progressed. By 1750 the Oriental motif dominated the decorative arts.

The export fan came to Europe in two forms, both traceable to Japan via China. The ancestor of the European brisé was the Japanese *hiogi*, probably developed from strips of wood, or *mokkan*, used as notebooks in the Nara period. The folding paper fan, known as the "bat" fan in Japan, was a logical development of the *hiogi*. By the tenth century, the *hiogi*, had appeared in China as the *che-san*, where it was first received with ridicule. By the fifteenth century, however, it had reached the hands of the Ming emperor Ch'eng Tsu.[1] The *hiogi*, or brisé form, never became popular in China, where the traditional form was the rigid-screen *pien-mien*. The hiogi was, however, a highly successful export. An export brisé of 1725 shows how Europeans appeared to the Chinese. The artist has emphasized their yellow hair and heavier bodies, and the rows of buttons on their clothes (cat. no. 22). A later fan in the collection, probably from the Netherlands, shows the cultural exchange in reverse (cat. no. 23). A Chinese sage, surrounded by attendants, meditates in his garden of oversize flowers. This was the image of a wise, peaceful China, an image in which war-weary Europe wished to believe and which, illusory or not, was to have the longest-lasting influence.

Collecting the rare, the valuable, and the exotic was the business of a monarch. In making China rooms in his European palace, the ruler was, in a way, extending his domain. Oriental ornament did not immediately appear on clothing, possibly because Louis XIV's dress code left no room for rival fantasy. Chinoiserie in costumes was, for the time, confined to frequent fancy dress balls, masquerades, and court masques such as one designed by Jean Berain. Chinoiserie ornament was even slow to appear on the fan, where gods and heroes echoed the heroics of the rule of the Sun King. Only toward the end of Louis XIV's reign do the landscapes of Cathay and its genial inhabitants infiltrate the corners and reserves of fans (cat. nos. 3 and 4). Not that chinoiserie was limited to things Chinese in inspiration; it generally came mixed with Japanese, Indian, and Persian elements. Even those few who knew the difference were unperturbed by the medley. Unhampered by ideas of historical accuracy, they had no difficulty accepting the presence of "Chinese" figures at the banquet of Mark Antony and Cleopatra (cat. no. 16).

The interim of the *Régence* (1715-23) between the death of Louis XIV and the accession of his great-grandson Louis XV witnessed a relaxation in manners, morals, and artistic expression. The removal of the court from Versailles to Paris after the Sun King's death meant a change of style on many levels. Straight lines gave way to the playful and capricious curves of the rococo, typified by the loose, floating gowns of the period. As intimacy replaced grandeur, all decoration was designed to be seen at close range. Because of their small size, fans were ideally suited to minute chinoiserie details. Small varnished brisés, made in the first quarter of the eighteenth century, exploited this kind of decoration with special brilliance (cat. no. 3). Their lustrous surfaces were a perfect foil for the Regency gowns, and the engaging figures of the chinoiserie repertory now seemed at home among the rocks and shells of the full-blown rococo. They gradually moved from the corners and reserves into the fans' central spaces. The stage was set for the fullest development of the fan in a society where appearance was all, and pleasure the only goal.

The noble pastoral is a recurrent human dream in which well-born, well-dressed young people exchange court or city artificiality for an unreal idyll in the country. Eighteenth-century Europe was still largely agricultural, and fan leaves regularly record the beauty of the open countryside. Aristocrats certainly made frequent visits to their country châteaux, but how much they indulged in rural make-believe when they arrived is not certain. Perhaps, like Count Hoditz (as reported by Max von Boehn) they trained their servants to act out pastoral scenes on their estates.[2] The artistic formula used repeatedly on fans placed a young woman in the center of the leaf, with an attentive young man at her feet. She was equipped with a few sheep and a beribboned *houlette* to keep them in line, he with a *musette* or a pastoral pipe. The full skirt of the shepherdess was always turned up to show a flirtatious, contrasting petticoat or was covered by an ornamental apron. A broad-brimmed hat completed her country costume. Her suitor generally wore some kind of costume reminiscent of the Italian comedy. Side figures performed such country tasks as watering plants, spinning wool, or fishing (cat. no. 48). Somewhere on the leaf or on the sticks one could expect to find chinoiserie. Cathay, after all, was another agricultural paradise devoted to leisure and refined sensuous enjoyment. Those gods and goddesses identified with the new values shared the manicured woods with the shepherds and shepherdesses: Venus, of course, Diana and the Muses, and any others whose depiction offered the school of Boucher an opportunity to paint the nude.

As France had dictated Europe's fashions since the time of Louis XIV, she now dictated the style of fans. With the popularity of hoop petticoats and then wide panniers that extended three feet on each side, fan proportions changed to describe a full half circle in order to balance the skirts (46.318, Appendix). But if French styles determined fan shapes, they did not always dictate the subject matter. Fans with stories from the Old Testament probably originated in the Netherlands or England, where they accompanied their owners to church (cat. no. 12).

Preoccupied with things of the present, people began to prefer fans with a contemporary focus, such as those decorated with the words and music of popular songs (cat. no. 68) or that recorded current events (cat. no. 30). Death occasionally intruded, but mourning did not require a woman of fashion to lay her fan aside: for those periods, special fans, painted in grisaille, were substituted (1976.211, Appendix). Since fashion's concerns are immediate, fans reflected current fads. When Josiah Child introduced his two-wheeled cabriolet in 1755, cabriolets appeared everywhere – on men's waistcoats, on ladies' caps, and, naturally, on fans (cat. no. 56; 1976.211 and 1976.212, Appendix).[3] The cab's prominent spokes may have encouraged the wider stick placement in fans in the last decades of the century. The first balloon ascensions created another furor. Everything was *au ballon*, including fans (1976.232, Appendix). Special fans commemorated events of importance, such as battles or royal births or weddings (cat. nos. 29 and 30). Printed fans, quickly produced, functioned almost like newspapers. Since England dominated the printed fan market, most commemorative fans were printed there and exported to France, Spain, and America. Advertisements for fans newly received from England appeared in Boston papers, for Boston was the center of the fan trade in colonial times.[4]

About mid-century, a subtle but unmistakable change in spirit occurred in Europe, like the turning of the seasons. Were people simply bored with pleasure? Had the excavations at Herculaneum and Pompeii raised questions about nobler values? Or was Jean-Jacques Rousseau responsible, with his disdain for the artificial and his worship of Nature? Madame de Pompadour's scented porcelain flowers at Bellevue might once have seemed remarkable and witty; it is unlikely that they stirred emotions. That, however, was the purpose of the gardens laid out at Kew Palace by Sir William Chambers. A ruined column, an altar, monument, or pagoda, standing in a garden of artful wildness, was intended to evoke a state of mind. The predictable courting scene is often set before a monument or altar borrowed from Sir William's so-called Anglo-Chinese garden.

It was suddenly good taste not only to have feelings but to show them. According to Max von Boehn, Frederick the Great burst into sobs upon reading particular French verses.[5] Fashion trivialized the new sensibility. The Duchess of Chartres wore a new coiffure that incorporated images of her children, birds, and servants, and called this creation her *pouf au sentiment*. For a time, feeling rested very much on the highly ornamented surface. Fan leaves made of silk complemented the crisp taffetas. Their widely spaced sticks gave an airy effect to leaves loaded with ornament. Sequins, chain-stitched gold thread, paint, and gilt made a rich showing above mother-of-pearl or ivory that was pierced, carved, painted, and gilded. Guard sticks acquired squared-off, heavy tops, carved and backed with foil – they looked not unlike the ladies in their soaring coiffures (cat. no. 51).

Just when French styles reached the height of luxury and frivolity, they were modified by a fresh breeze from across the Channel. Increasing English influence led the way to simpler styles, both in costumes and in fans. A greater number of fans both in France and England were mounted *à l'anglaise*, that is, with ribs glued directly to the reverse of a single leaf. The leaves carried decreasing amounts of ornament, the inner sticks were now severely plain, and even the guards were decoratively restrained, with lighter gilding. Typically, a central medallion by an artist such as Angelica Kauffmann might have a surrounding design in the classicizing style of the Adam brothers (cat. no. 20). Anglomania was more than a fashionable caprice. Acceptance of a new social and artistic style went along with the Marlborough hats and redingotes (riding coats) worn in France. The new style, developed in England before becoming popular in France, originally had been inspired by Italy. Two generations of rich young Englishmen had been traveling to Italy to absorb ancient culture as part of their education. Their exposure to clas-

sical monuments and statuary inspired architecture and interior decoration at home. Straight, clean lines replaced rococo curves and expressed the new morality of a society in a reforming mood. All European fans became simpler in style, but in France they also deteriorated in materials and finish. Craftsmanship per se came under suspicion as a part of the old regime and an attribute of privilege. The fan itself, inescapably associated with coquetry, symbolized an attitude morally unacceptable to zealous reformers. Some printed fans carried the words of revolutionary songs (cat. no. 71), others showed sympathy for the royal family, but these were no longer perceived as objects of value. The great days of the fan industry were over.

Attrition of the industry was followed by a dwindling in the size of fans themselves, until they were small enough to justify the name "imperceptibles" (43.2092, Appendix). The shrinkage of both industry and product represented fashion's response to political and social change. The clinging gowns worn by the *merveilleuses* made impractical the separate pockets that had been invisible under a pannier, in which a fan might be carried. Women in the Directoire and Empire modes had their hands quite full enough carrying reticules (from *ridicules*) and manipulating the Kashmir shawls that kept them from freezing. Fans, if carried, were of the small brisé type made of horn or had fabric leaves bright with sequins and spangles. The large-leaved fan painted with a figural scene disappeared for a generation.

The small horn fans of the 1820s were usually blond, occasionally darkened to imitate tortoiseshell. They were decorated with piqué work of inlaid metal dots, some-

16

times combined with painting and gilding. The blades often ended in points resembling the crockets of the neo-Gothic churches springing up all over England (43.2095, Appendix). Some continued to surround their subjects with classical decoration (1976.330, Appendix), while others anticipated the Romantic style soon to dominate contemporary costumes (1976.248, Appendix).

The new mood of nostalgia was reinforced by an elaborate ball given by the Duchesse de Berry in 1829, to which guests were required to wear historical costumes. The ball started a vogue for reprises which continued for most of the century. Old fans were in demand, and since the supply was inadequate, especially in France, a new industry sprang up specializing in copies. Some of these were actually sold as authentic; others copied old forms, such as the *Hawking Party* (1976.189, Appendix) or *The Engagement* (cat. no. 74), or used old subject matter without intending to deceive (cat. no. 79). Fashion followed the same course, reviving eighteenth-century styles with tight corsetry and hoop skirts. Ladies in crinolines held large gilded fans showing beaux and belles in powdered wigs, leaving no doubt as to the imitative nature of both costumes and fans.

Although very elegant paper-leaved fans with rococo or Empire themes continued to be produced by such prestigious houses as Duvelleroy (cat. no. 78), the trend toward textile leaves grew stronger after the middle of the nineteenth century. Leaves echoed the sumptuous textiles, heavy satins, and lace and feather trimming characteristic of the gowns of Charles Frederick Worth. Hats and fans sprouted feathers with tiny whole birds attached as ornaments (63.663, Appendix). Lace combined with silk gauze was painted with the usual flowers, cupids, and occasional figures (cat. no. 84). Fan painting, like china painting, was approved as an amateur hobby. Debutantes and young girl graduates carried simple, lace-trimmed fans with painted decoration. White satin fans, painted with roses, lilies of the valley, and forget-me-nots, were reserved for brides.

Unexpectedly, the Japanese prints that inspired the Impressionists may have changed the attitude of painters toward the fan form. Degas and others produced a small number of paintings in that format.[6] Mainstream fans remained costume accessories, but they, too, took new directions. Daring shapes were introduced, such as that of *Baroque Feathers* (1976.516, Appendix). Fans borrowed theatricality from the Ballets Russes, inventiveness from Poiret (cat. no. 100). It seemed that new life stirred in the old form. Then, suddenly, World War I struck midnight for this Cinderella object, which abruptly disappeared from the ballroom and resumed an inglorious and utilitarian role. Postwar society was moving too fast for the fan, and women's roles had changed. The fashion-conscious person held a cocktail or a cigarette; those more seriously inclined picked up the banner of the suffragette.

1. See the Fan Circle, in association with the Victoria and Albert Museum, *Fans from the East* (London, 1978), pp. 29, 37.

2. See Max von Boehn, *Modes and Manners*, trans. Joan Joshua (London, 1935), vol. 4, p. 138.

3. See George Woolliscroft Rhead, *History of the Fan* (Philadelphia, 1910), p. 164.

4. See Katherine Morris Lester and Bess Viola Oerke, *Accessories of Dress* (Peoria, Ill., 1940), p. 451.

5. See von Boehn, *Modes and Manners*, p. 70.

6. See Monika Kopplin, *Kompositionen im Halbrund* (Stuttgart-Zurich, 1984).

THE "ALMOST INCREDIBLE COMMERCE":

The Marketing and Manufacture of Fans

In his *Universal Dictionary of Commerce*, republished in 1760, Jacques Savary called the French fan trade "Le commerce . . . presque incroyable," not only supplying the needs of Paris and the provinces but also sending an even greater number outside the country annually. Spain, England, and Holland were the principal, but not necessarily the final, destinations. The bulk of shipments were then dispersed from these points to America and to the northern and Baltic Sea markets (i.e., Flanders, Scandinavia, and Russia).[1]

However great the French output, quantities of fans were also entering the country from China and England. These were typically fans of considerable value. In 1699 the *Macclesfield* sailed from Canton with a cargo that included 100,000 fans.[2] The English East India Company instructed its representatives to look for fine lacquerware and to supply Chinese fan-makers with patterns to follow. The French product, known for its delicacy and grace, was admittedly surpassed by the imports in two respects: by China's lacquer and by the beauty of English sticks. Chinese fans sometimes reached England by irregular routes developed by privateers. English pirates in the Pacific frequently intercepted galleons from Manila loaded with goods bound for Spain via Mexico. One Manilan prize yielded a substantial 5,806 fans.[3]

An exotic flavor, the mystique of a foreign culture, was essential to the fashion of the fan. Even the materials of which fans were made came from great distances: ivory from India or Africa; mother-of-pearl from Madagascar, Sydney, Sumatra; tortoiseshell from Borneo, Bali, and Guinea. All were brought to Canton to be carved. Ivory was the favored stick material, obtained from the tusks of elephants. African elephants had longer tusks, some measuring up to eight feet, but Indian ivory was preferred as being whiter and easier to carve. Italians had mastered the art of ivory carving in the seventeenth century and the French learned from them; yet it was acknowledged that the finest sticks came from China. Mother-of-pearl, the iridescent lining of pearl oyster shells, built up in layers, rivaled ivory as a luxury material for the sticks. Among the many varieties available, the striking white *poulette* from Madagascar was outstanding, as was the "black" pearl from Sydney with its bluish cast. Iridescent shells are found in all seas, but the kind known as "goldfish" from Japan was the most spectacular. Like ivory, mother-of-pearl was worked with fine blades and little saws. Stick-makers in the *département* of l'Oise, between Méru and Beauvais, softened it with dilute sulphuric acid to facilitate carving.

Pinpointing a fan's place of origin is complicated by the fact that not only materials but also finished fan parts and the skilled workmen themselves moved about as the trade demanded. Samuel Redgrave described this phenomenon in his catalogue of the fan exhibition held at the South Kensington Museum in 1870: "Workmen of one country have been tempted to another; Chinese carvers brought to Europe; parts of fans in which a particular country has excelled have been imported to another, and used with its native manufacture."[4]

Piecemeal production and a composite product marked French fans as well as imports. Guild restrictions limited craftsmen to one material or to one process. Since fans were made of materials as disparate as paper and shell, ivory and feathers, skin and metal, it was inevitable that a fan should be the work of many hands. Although fans were in general use throughout the seventeenth century, the regulations governing their manufacture did not crystallize until the century's end. Until that time, the right to make a fan was contested by the members of the leather gilders, the merchants, and the painters. Louis XIV's edict of 1673 made leaf makers a corporate body (*éventaillistes*), and their privileges were extended in 1676 and 1678. These specialists were forbidden to make fan sticks; this work fell to the *tabletiers*, carvers of small ivory objects such as chessmen, crucifixes, and snuffboxes. The separation of function usually meant a physical separation as well, since common interests drew artisans together into villages dominated by a single craft. French fan leaves were painted in Paris and the fans assembled there, but the sticks might have come from any one of the many *tabletier* villages located in the *département* of l'Oise or even from far-off China, while most of the gilding was done by specialists in Dieppe.

Such rigid segregation does not seem to have been the case in England. When arms were granted to the Worshipful Company of Fan Makers in 1709, the words "or Fanstick-makers" were added in the *Minute Book of the Company*. Their shield showed not only a completed fan but the tools of the fan stick-makers: the shaver for thinning the ivory, the saw for the pierced fretwork. Neither the palette nor the brushes of the leaf painter were included.[5]

Whether domestic or imported, the sticks were sent to Paris, where the leaves were prepared, painted, and eventually united with the sticks for the finished product. The *Encyclopédie* of Diderot and d'Alembert describes and illustrates the successive steps through which paper passed on its way to becoming a fan leaf. First, two sheets were glued together, then stretched, dried on a semicircular frame, and trimmed to prepare them for the painter. The painting of the leaf was followed by scoring on a mold with a small metal tool to establish the pleat lines. With folding on the lines and trimming completed, the leaf was ready for the sticks. A passage had to be opened for the rib (the upper portion of the stick) by inserting a copper probe after each pleat between the front and back layer of the glued double leaf. The sticks could then be eased into the prepared channels and the top edge finished, if desired, with a band.

Although the majority of fan leaves were made of paper and painted in gouache, finely prepared skin was a frequent early choice, especially in Italy. The skins were painted, printed from an engraved plate, or cut out in a lacy design, découpage being an Italian specialty (cat. nos. 1 and 53). The reign of Louis XV is usually held to be the era during which the art of the fan-maker reached its perfection, but the preceding decades were in some ways more exciting because of the experimentation being carried out. Stick-makers were combining new materials and new techniques were developing: pearl panels fastened on ivory, ivory decorated with silver piqué. The artists who painted the leaves drew their imagery from an equally eclectic mix of baroque, classical, and contemporary literary and pictorial sources, all sauced with the exoticism of the Orient as it was perceived. The typical leaf of the early period was dark in color, and the scene was painted straight across the leaf without any reference to its curve (although Abraham Bosse's designs had made this advance a century earlier [cat. no. 4 and frontispiece, 1976.568]). The painters often based their designs on easel paintings or engravings made from paintings.

A certain brilliant type of ivory brisé fan made a brief trajectory in the first quarter of the eighteenth century and was revived in the nineteenth. The ivory blades, held together by a connecting ribbon, were first oil painted with intricate ornamentation, then heavily gilded and varnished. Varnish had been developed as a substitute for the Oriental lacquer, which was unobtainable in Europe.[6] Experimental work had been carried out and published in England,[7] and Venice had been producing fine "lacquered" (i.e., varnished) surfaces since the seventeenth century. Soon France and the Netherlands as well were creating these lustrous fans. The continuing expansion of the fan industry and the export of fans and fan parts from France, England, Italy, and the Netherlands assured the dissemination of techniques and styles.

In 1760, at the peak of their production, fans were still made entirely by hand. But there was some evidence that attempts were afoot to devise shortcuts to meet the enormous demands of the industry.[8] That same year, Edouard Petit of the Paris fan-making house of Ducrot & Petit improved on the pleating mold, obviating much of the need for tedious hand pleating and speeding up production.[9] Increasingly, sticks were pierced and then painted or encrusted with silver leaf, replacing the arduous carving, piqué, and inlay work. The silver leaf was applied to the sticks by means of *la drogue*, a substance that, according to Savary, the stick-makers tried to make very mysterious, but which was no more than a mixture of gum arabic, rock sugar, honey dissolved in water, and alcohol (*eau de vie*).[10] There was also a movement to tighten up the industry by uniting the painters, carvers, and varnish workers by a royal edict in 1775.

The industry clung to this pinnacle of success for a decade, then began to falter about 1770 and decline in quality. A flood of cheap and attractive printed fans from England encroached on the French trade and took work away from the fan painters, as did the trend toward textile leaves. The painted areas of fans shrank to vignettes on paper, silk, or lace. Sequins sewn to the leaf provided quick and easy decoration. The simplification process was most noticeable on the sticks, which were stripped of ornament below the shoulder. At the same time, the downgrading of material and manufacture proceeded. Greek and Roman scenes were popular fan subjects in the uneasy first years of the Republic (1792-93). These were followed by *négligé à la patriote*. This meant patriotic rags for the men, cheap fans for the women.[11] The course of the French Revolution can be followed in the decline of the fan industry which soon was in ruins, partly because luxury items were politically dangerous, partly because of the change in dress styles. Two-thirds of the fan-makers of Paris were said to have been forced out of business when women started to carry reticules. The small, leafless brisés of bone, ivory, wood, cardboard, metal, skin, and horn, especially, filled the leanest days of the industry, between 1809 and 1815.

The second era of the fan industry coincided with the Restoration (of the monarchy) and with the attempt to recapture the spirit and brilliance of the *ancien régime.* Symptomatic of this desire was the Duchesse de Berry's famous costume ball of 1829, organized as three quadrilles, the third of which was Louis XV style. The antique shop of the perfumer Vanier, on the rue Caumartin, was ransacked for appropriate fans for the occasion. These elegant antiques were instrumental in returning the large-leaved pictorial fan to favor and bringing a reprieve to the moribund industry.

While Vanier collected and sold old fans, his partner, the artist Desrochers, used them as models for reproduction, an effort continued by his son-in-law, Alexandre. The Gimbel brothers of Strasbourg also had a thriving business of reproducing old fans, which flourished from 1846 to 1851.[12] Subsequent development of the industry illustrated the difficulty of re-creating a past era with contemporary technology. Spire Blondel, in his 1875 history of fans described "several industrial improvements which had a favorable influence on production in general and notably on those articles of modest cost."[13] These "improvements" had the double goal of reducing hand-work and finding substitutes for expensive materials – the ultimate goals of mechanization in all industries. The goals were met, but the result could not equal the handmade fan of the eighteenth century.

Changes appeared first on the fan leaf. As hand-colored intaglio prints from engraved plates had to some extent replaced paintings in gouache, so lithographs began to take the place of hand-colored prints after 1829. Mechanical carving perfected by Alphonse Baude in 1859, was the next invention to change the industry. This machine made open grillwork a feature even of inexpensive fans, but at the price of excessive regularity and monotony. About a decade later, the American fan-maker, Edmund Soper Hunt, of Weymouth Landing, Massachusetts, took out a patent for a machine that assembled sticks, leaf, and rivet in one operation, completing the mechanization of fan production.[14]

Familiarity with the new materials and processes that were coming into use in the nineteenth century can be valuable in determining the date of manufacture. Identification is not always easy. Horn, celluloid, and even bone masqueraded as tortoiseshell. Bone or celluloid (nitrated cellulose) stood in for ivory. Japanned papier-mâché posed as lacquerware. In order to distinguish between the true and false, one must keep in mind the physical properties of the original materials as well as the traditional ways in which they were worked. These should be compared with the appearance of possible substitutes and their respective machining.

The precious material known as tortoiseshell had been admired and used for luxury products since Roman times. It is made from the protective cover of the smallest of the sea turtles, the *Chelonia imbricata* or "hawksbill" turtle found in the western Pacific from the eastern archipelago and the east coast of Celebes to New Guinea. The turtle has thirteen plates on its back, five large central ones, and four smaller ones on each side. The plates differ from horn in that their fibrous structure is apparent only under magnification, but they can be worked in exactly the same way. The routine steps in their preparation include straightening and flattening by immersion in a hot-water bath, then pressing and cooling between sheets of metal or hardwood. The plates can be used separately or welded together by aligning them and plunging them into boiling water. Scrapings are saved, put into metallic molds with small pieces, and, again, treated with heat and pressure until a compact mass of "melted shell" is obtained. This homogenous tissue can be cut and polished in all directions.

Tortoiseshell is most successfully imitated by horn, to which it is chemically related, both being modified forms of epidermic tissue, albuminoid keratin. Ox horns, animal hooves, claws, and nails, tortoise carapaces, porcupine quills, and bird feathers are all related proteinaceous materials. For fans, flattened sections of horn or scraps of horn and hooves, boiled and reformed under pressure, were either pressed or cast in metallic molds. Markings similar to those of natural tortoiseshell could be added by staining the horn with various solutions: silver in *aqua regia* (nitric and hydrochloric acids) for a red color, silver in nitric acid for black, mercury in nitric acid for brown. These solutions, applied on the natural yellow of horn, imitated true shell so successfully that detection was virtually impossible, except for the fact that the false shell was a little less transparent and softer.

Careful inspection can sometimes reveal how the material was worked. Diagonal striations on the sticks, for example, may indicate turning and grinding on a lap wheel. Flashing on the sides may show where halves of a mold met, although care was usually taken to remove these signs. The shell-like markings applied to horn are sometimes signaled by excessive regularity. The "Neapolitan shell" sold by antiques dealers usually is imitation shell made from horn.

Celluloid and related early plastics were made from cellulose fibers nitrated and mixed with camphor. The resulting gel, made into blocks under high pressure and temperatures, could be machined, molded, or pressed into shape. Celluloid came into use in the 1860s and it was used extensively until the 1950s, when newer plastics replaced it. Chemical laboratory tests can identify celluloid without difficulty. For a simpler test, it has been claimed that a celluloid surface rubbed with a soft cloth may give off a detectable camphor odor. In addition, celluloid is characteristically shiny.

The naked eye immediately registers a color difference between ivory and its imposters. Bone appears too white when compared to the range of warm tones possible with ivory. This characteristic of bone is accentuated by the whiting routinely applied to it during manufacture. The growth lines of ivory (annular, in section) look very different from the Haversian canals that carry blood vessels and nerves in the living bone. These appear later as voids usually filled in with a colorless gelatinous substance subsequently disguised by whiting. This filling can darken with age or drop out, leaving dark vertical lines or holes.

The imitation ivory sticks made by the American fanmaker Edmund Soper Hunt were much admired. His process was kept secret, but it seems probable that bone was the basis, boiled or limed, filled and whitened, and polished on lap wheels. He might also have started with ground bone and mixed it with gelatine and alum for a product that could be pressed and formed in steel molds. Designs pressed into the material in a softened state will show rounded edges and will lack the crispness characteristic of carved ivory.

The lacquered sticks of the Orient were imitated by japanned papier-mâché. This type of work, of which there is a fine example in the museum's collection (cat. no. 76), recalls an industry that flourished in England between 1825 and 1860. Improvements in the japanning process had been made in the eighteenth century by John Baskerville and Henry Clay, who used papier-mâché panels as support for the japanning previously applied to tinware. Sheets of unsized rag paper were pasted with cooked glue and flour and waterproofed with linseed oil. The resulting material could be worked like wood. It was painted, gilded, and finished with an alcohol-based varnish that gave it a hard and shiny surface. In 1825 the firm of Jennens and Bettridge developed a means of embellishing japanned design with mother-of-pearl. Those parts of the design to be pearl covered were stenciled with asphaltum and the pearl sheet was dipped in acid. Everything not covered with asphaltum dissolved, leaving the shapes needed for the design. These were applied while the varnish was still tacky. The popularity of japanned papier-mâché peaked with the Great Exhibition of 1851 and declined soon thereafter.[14]

The typical eighteenth-century paper fan, when held against the light, will show the laid lines and chain lines of antique laid paper.[15] These markings were made when the paper was formed from rag pulp on the paper-maker's screen, and they were not easy to counterfeit, although this was attempted in the nineteenth century. Skin, also widely used in the old fans, was imitated by what came to be called "chicken-skin paper." The paper was given a similar surface by impressing it with a follicle pattern simulating the holes left in a skin after the hair has been removed. Sometimes this pattern seems too regular to be authentic, or its scale is disproportionate to the size of the "skin." Careful examination of any damaged area will reveal whether the follicle pattern is more than superficial. In addition, the paper leaf will tend to be thinner than a skin leaf and will appear more brittle in areas of wear, such as the edges of the folds. Differentiation can be made positively in the laboratory under the microscope if fiber samples are available.

The art of enhancing natural materials was carried to extremes in the case of mother-of-pearl. Cutting it on an angle was found to create a rippled effect. It was occasionally dyed unnatural colors, such as bright yellow or green, or its natural iridescence was accentuated by the application of heat or chemicals.[16]

The fans of two centuries in the Museum of Fine Arts' collection bear witness to the art of the fan-maker in exploiting the beauty of natural materials and, when these became scarce or prohibitively costly, finding substitutes in the discoveries of a new age. The skill of the artist/craftsman emerges as the truly incredible part of an amazing industry.

Disparate qualities and skills mark the three periods of

fan production. Seamanship and enterprise brought the first foreign fans to Europe, where they gave rise to a prodigious industry. The manual skills of native craftsmen fueled that industry, enabling it to supply the demands of an elite society. Finally, the manufacturers' ingenuity created machines and synthetics to bring down costs. It brought down commerce as well, however, for the prestige of the luxury item disappeared when "progress" brought it within every woman's reach.

1. Jacques Savary des Bruslons, *Dictionnaire universel de commerce* (Copenhagen, 1760), vol. 2, p. 478.

2. See J. B. da Silva, "Chinese Fans and the Porcelain Trade with the West," *Fans: Bulletin of the Fan Circle International* 19 (Autumn 1981): 21-26.

3. See Brian Little, "Fans on the High Seas," *Fans* 18 (Summer 1981): 26.

4. Redgrave, in G. Woolliscroft Rhead, *History of the Fan* (Philadelphia, 1910), p. 150.

5. See MacIver Percival, *The Fan Book* (London, 1920), pp. 222-23.

6. The *Rhus vernicifera* tree, source of Oriental lacquer, would not grow in Europe.

7. See John Stalker and George Parker, *A Treatise of Japanning and Varnishing, 1688*, intro. by H. D. Molesworth (Levittown, N.Y., 1972).

8. In 1753 there were one hundred and fifty fan-makers in Paris.

9. See Cooper-Hewitt Museum, *Folding Fans*. (Catalogue by Lucy A. Commoner), Washington, D.C., 1986, p. 13.

10. See Savary, *Dictionnaire universel de commerce*, p. 478.

11. See Spire Blondel, *Histoire des éventails* (Paris, 1875), p. 146.

12. Ibid., pp. 179-80.

13. Ibid.

14. See Esther Oldham, "American Victorian Fans: 'Allen Fans,' " part 1, *The Antiques Journal* (August 1953): 21-22.

15. See Dianne van der Reyden and Donald C. Williams, "The Technology and Conservation of a Nineteenth Century English Chair," *Preprints* (Papers presented at the Fourteenth Annual Meeting of the American Institute for Conservation of Historic and Artistic Works, Chicago, May 21-23, 1986).

16. See Dard Hunter, *Papermaking: The History and Technique of an Ancient Craft* (New York, 1974), fig. 94, p. 115.

17. Emil Schnorr, interview with the author, September 5, 1986; letter to the author, October 28, 1986.

ANNOTATED ENTRIES

Author's Note

Dates and artists' names rarely appear on eighteenth-century fans, except for the printed variety required to include such information. The migration of craftsmen and the import of foreign fan parts similarly obscure questions of provenance.

The dates and countries of origin assigned to each catalogue entry rest mainly on comparative study, internal evidence, and the recorded opinions of visiting authorities (who were not always in agreement). It is hoped that the catalogue will stimulate new studies, making greater accuracy possible.

Esther Oldham's magnificent gift of June 9, 1976, tripled the size of the Museum of Fine Arts' existing fan collection. In order to avoid repetition, the acknowledgment line for entries in the Catalogue and Appendix, unless otherwise noted, will be understood as "Gift of Esther Oldham."

I Literary Themes

Contrary to a widely held notion that interest in the classics developed late in the eighteenth century, many earlier fans show a broad familiarity with Greek and Roman subjects, including relatively obscure classical stories. Scenes from ancient history, mythology, and romance were usually painted straight across the leaf, in the manner of the paintings or engravings from which most of them derive.

Fans with Old Testament themes were considered appropriate accessories for the churchgoer. Many such fans were made in the Netherlands, although at least one in the present group is English. They offer a study in variety, from the naive charm of *Moses Striking the Rock* to the sophisticated manner of the Joseph story, told in high rococo vignettes.

Ivory guard stick, (cat. 12)
Netherlands, c. 1750
1976.321

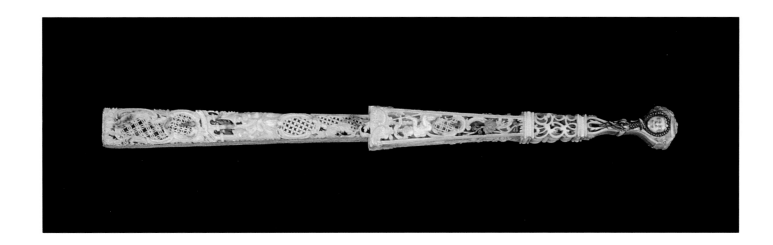

The Legend of Marcus Curtius (cat. 1)

England or southern Netherlands, mid-17th century
Engraved skin leaf
18 ivory sticks (some bone replacements), tortoiseshell and mother-of-pearl panels on guards
Guard: 28 cm. Maximum open: 47.5 cm. Arc: 135° Acc. no. 1976.290

In the scene engraved on this fan, a portion of the Coliseum and a Roman temple front define the location as the Roman Forum. A young horseman, fully armed, charges toward a chasm into which women are throwing jewels and other precious objects. The horseman is Marcus Curtius, the time 362 B.C. According to legend, a deep abyss had opened up in the middle of the Forum. An oracle predicted it would close with the sacrifice of that which Rome valued most highly. Interpreting this to mean that Rome must sacrifice its youth and its soldiers, Curtius galloped into the void, which closed above him, leaving only a small lake.[1]

A heavy baroque border surrounds the scene with animals and semihuman figures caught in decorative iron strapwork. This motif can be traced to the sixteenth century, but the engraving is certainly no earlier than mid-seventeenth century.

On the guard, tortoiseshell plates with piqué work alternate with plates of incised mother-of-pearl. The guard terminates in a seamonster's head, its eye at the rivet.

1. The artist's literary source may have been Valerius Maximus, *Facta Dictaque Memorabilia*, bk. 5, chap. 6:2, where, under the title "De Pietate erga Patriam," Curtius is cited as an exemplar of patriotism.

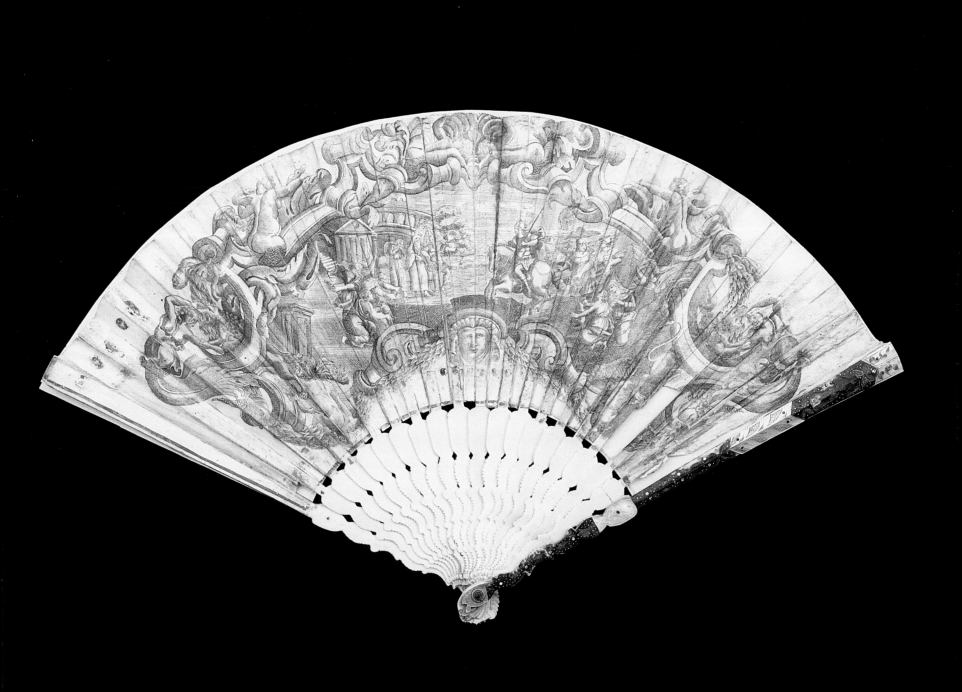

Achilles at Skyros (cat. 2)

France (?), 1720s
Brisé fan, 28 thin ivory blades, painted in oil and varnished
Discontinuous painted silk connecting ribbon
Mother-of-pearl thumbguard and washer
Guard: 21 cm. Maximum open: 36.5 cm. Arc: 120° Acc. no. 17.166
Gift of Mrs. Winthrop Sargent

The post-Homeric episode of Achilles at the court of Lyco-medes is painted in soft greens and grays and enclosed by a green-gold frame. The oracle Kalchas predicted that Troy could not be taken without Achilles but that the hero would die in the attack. To avoid this fate, Achilles was concealed for a time at Skyros, among the daughters of King Lycomedes. Achilles in women's clothing leans on a shield as he looks toward the helmet offered him by Ulysses, who is disguised as a peddler. The peddler's mirror and jewels attract the daughters of Lycomedes, but Achilles' eye is caught by the armor. His interest reveals his identity, and he can no longer avoid involvement in the Trojan War. His destiny, as well as that of Troy, is sealed.[1]

In spite of considerable paint loss, this early brisé fan retains much of its superb quality. Its subject matter, restraint, and elegance mark it as intended for an educated and discriminating clientele.

1. See Wolfgang Stechow, "A Modello by Jacob Jordaens," *Allen Memorial Art Museum Bulletin* 23 (Fall 1965): 5-16. Stechow has traced this rather inglorious episode in the Achilles story to the sixteenth-century Italian scholar Natale Conti.

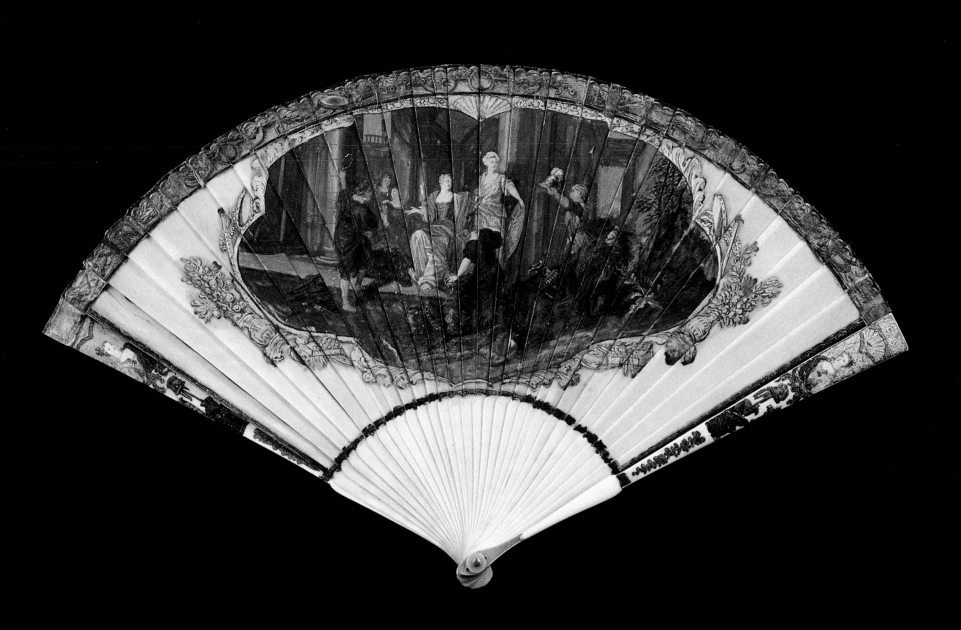

King Solomon
and the Queen of Sheba (cat. 3)

Netherlands (?), c. 1720s
Brisé fan, 28 ivory blades, painted in oil and varnished
Blue silk connecting ribbon at top edge
Tortoiseshell thumbguard, mother-of-pearl washer
Guard: 21.5 cm. Maximum open: 35.5 cm. Arc: 120°
Acc. no. 1976.188

In the biblical story of the meeting of King Solomon and the Queen of Sheba (II Chronicles 9:1-9), the queen comes to test the wisdom of the fabled Solomon and leaves convinced that his fame is justified. On this fan, the scene occupies the central space, surrounded by an angular frame of black and gold. This rather spiky frame shape may have been intended to extend the Oriental theme illustrated in the many small reserves spaced symmetrically over the orange-red and gold ground. Both the principals wear crowns. Solomon extends his hand in greeting. The visiting queen points to her servants bearing rich gifts.

On the reverse, similarly framed, a woman and her train bearer stand on a pier, waving farewell to a departing ship.

The vignettes in the reserves, blue on pale blue or lavender on lavender, resemble scenes on blue-and-white export porcelain.

32

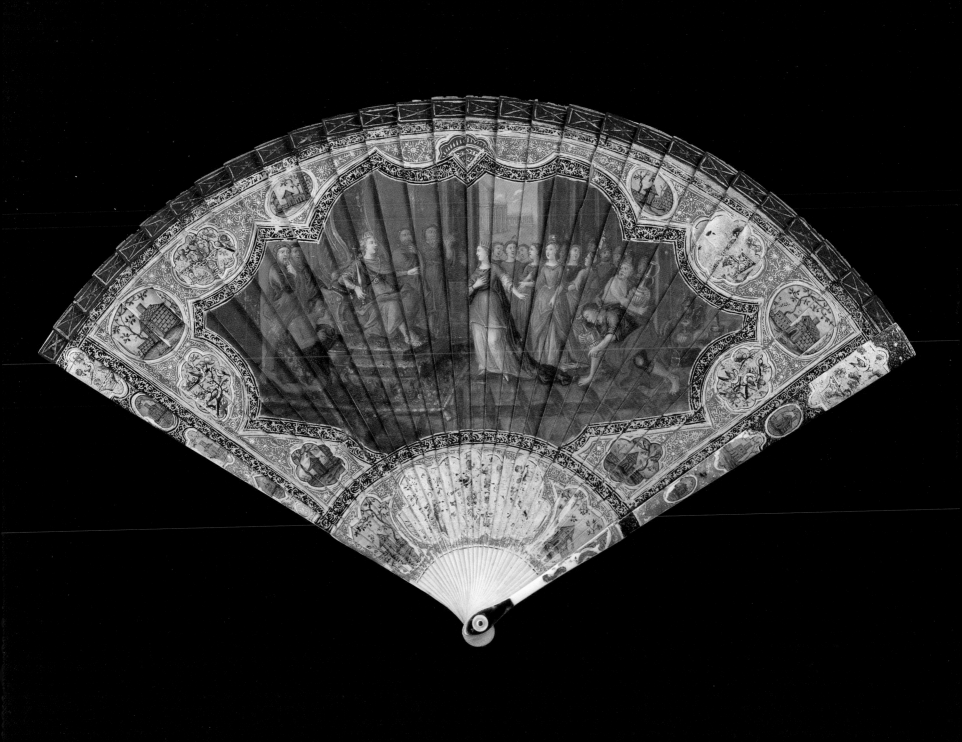

The Accusation of Tuccia (cat. 4)

France, 1720s
Leaf: skin recto, paper verso, painted in gouache
20 ivory sticks, pierced and carved with applied mother-of-pearl panels
Large mother-of-pearl thumbguard and washer
Guard: 28 cm. Maximum open: 49 cm. Arc: 145° Acc. no. 1976.202

A magical statue of the goddess Pallas Athena stood in the temple of Vesta in Rome, where vestal virgins carried out their ritual worship. It was believed that the goddess would be incensed if her statue was touched by "impure" hands, and the safety of Rome would be jeopardized. A vestal accused of losing her virginity was required to carry water in a sieve from the Tiber to the temple of Vesta to prove her innocence.

The painting shows a vestal named Tuccia on trial. She wears the crown of flowers and the bridal gown prescribed for priestesses. Her accuser is shown handing her the sieve with which she must perform the test. Tuccia appealed to the goddess Vesta and carried the water successfully.[1] Regarded as an exemplar of chastity, Tuccia was the subject of many paintings in the baroque and rococo periods.[2]

Blue-and-white chinoiserie reserves interrupt a border of pink and gold. Mother-of-pearl panels, attached to the guards rather than laminated, may account for the guards' marked warping.

1. See Valerius Maximus, *Facta Dictaque Memorabilia*, bk. 8, chap. 1:5 (Leiden, 1726), p. 699, and Pliny, *Natural History*, bk. 28, chap. 3:12.

2. See Andres Pigler, *Barockthemen* (Budapest, 1965), vol. 2, pp. 332-34, 418-19.

The Rape of Europa (cat. 5)

France or Italy, 1700-25
Skin leaf (single), painted in gouache
20 ivory sticks with delicate piqué work
Large mother-of-pearl thumbguard and washer
Guard: 26.5 cm. Maximum open: 48 cm. Arc: 150° Acc. no. 1976.340

In depicting this subject, Italian artists usually chose a less passive moment, typically showing the bull rushing into the sea with the frightened girl on his back. Here Europa, surrounded by her companions, sits on the back of a peaceful bull who placidly allows himself to be decorated with garlands. The animal's human eyes betray the fact that he is Zeus in disguise. Two naked *putti* play near the water's edge, while a naiad watches from the extreme left. A finely painted Mediterranean landscape stretches out into the distance to the right.

Flowering branches, gracefully arranged, cover the entire reverse, effectively concealing the supporting sticks. The guard sticks have a delicate floral design picked out in silver piqué.

Exhibitions
Fans from the Oldham Collection, Museum of Fine Arts, Boston, November 25, 1977 - March 5, 1978.

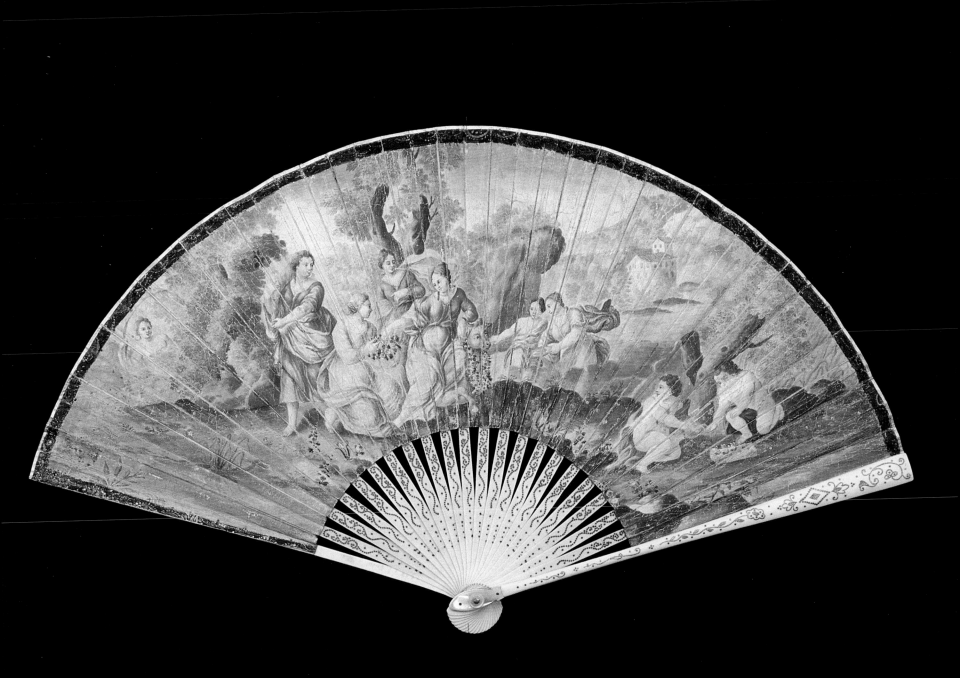

Theseus at the Court of Aegeus *(cat. 6)*

Italy (Venice), c. 1725
Leaf: skin recto, paper verso, painted in gouache
18 ivory sticks, painted, gilded, and inlaid with mother-of-pearl[1]
Mother-of-pearl thumbguards and button at rivet
Guard: 29 cm. Maximum open: 53 cm. Arc: 150° Acc. no. 1976.201

At a table set in an outdoor pavilion, a king sits with a young woman and a warrior in a plumed helmet. The king warns his guest not to drink from the goblet he holds as the woman watches intently. It is the dramatic moment at which Aegeus, king of Athens, recognizes his son Theseus by his sword and prevents him from drinking the poison prepared by his wicked stepmother, the witch Medea.

The sticks are particularly fine. A central cartouche, painted on mother-of-pearl, shows three figures with bagpipe, falcon, and *houlette*. A shepherdess with a *houlette*

decorates the guard. An upper border of delicate tracery with triangular shapes is similar to the border of the fan depicting *Rinaldo in the Garden of Armida* (cat. no. 8) and to a fan in the Messel-Rosse collection, now at the Fitzwilliam Museum in Cambridge, England.[2]

1. Avril Hart of the Victoria and Albert Museum noted on a visit to the MFA in 1983 that varnish had been applied at a later date.

2. See Nancy Armstrong, *Fans from the Fitzwilliam* (Cambridge, 1985), no. 10, "Venetian, c. 1730."

The Family of Darius Before Alexander (cat. 7)

France, 1720-40
After the painting by Charles LeBrun (1661), engraved by G. Edelinck or Simon Gribelin (c. 1671)[1]
Skin leaf (single), painted in watercolor, lightly gilded
20 ivory sticks, delicately carved and pierced; guards carved and painted
Guard: 27.5 cm. Maximum open: 45.5 cm. Arc: 125° Acc. no. 01.6685
Bequest of Mrs. Arthur Croft

Alexander the Great invaded Persia in 334 B.C. After the decisive battle of Issus in 333, King Darius's wife, mother, and children were taken prisoner, although Darius himself escaped. When Alexander came to the royal tent to see the prisoners, he was accompanied by his friend Hephaistion. The women prostrated themselves before the taller man, in error, but Alexander magnanimously dismissed their mistake. He raised Sisigambis, the mother of Darius, to her feet, and ordered all the women's ornaments returned to them.[2]

French painter Charles LeBrun (1619-1690) solidified his position in the court of Louis XIV with his first commission, *The Family of Darius Before Alexander,* since the king felt a kinship with the Greek hero. From this date, LeBrun received all the most important commissions.[3] Gérard Edelinck, who may have engraved this fan, was also in the service of Louis XIV, who settled a pension on him. His bold and finished execution was worked entirely with the graver.[4]

The Gobelins tapestry woven after an engraving of LeBrun's painting follows it closely, except for the addition of a great deal of foliage. The fan designer, limited by the leaf's horizontal format, eliminated the ornate top of the tent and moved the seated spectator farther from the group. There is some correspondence between the colors in the tapestry and those of the fan, although the adherence is not strict. Both tapestry and fan are oriented in the same direction as the painting, while the engraving is reversed.

1. See Edith A. Standen, *European Post-Medieval Tapestries and Related Hangings in the Metropolitan Museum of Art,* 2 vols. (New York, 1985), vol. 1, no. 37a, pp. 232-234, ill. p. 233.

2. See Quintus Curtius, *History of Alexander,* trans. John C. Rolfe (London, 1946), bk. 3, chap. 12: 13-23, cited in Standen, ibid.

3. See Anthony Blunt, *Art and Architecture in France 1500-1700* (Harmondsworth, England), p. 243, plate 164A; and Donald Posner, "Charles Lebrun's *Triumph of Alexander,*" *Art Bulletin* 41 (1959): 237-48.

4. See *Bryan's Dictionary of Painters and Engravers* (London, 1919).

Exhibitions

The Search for Alexander, Museum of Fine Arts, Boston, October 23, 1981 – January 10, 1982, and The Fine Arts Museums of San Francisco, M. H. de Young Museum, February 19-May 16, 1982.

Publications

The Search for Alexander: Supplement II to the Catalogue (Boston, 1981), p. 20, no. 31, ill.

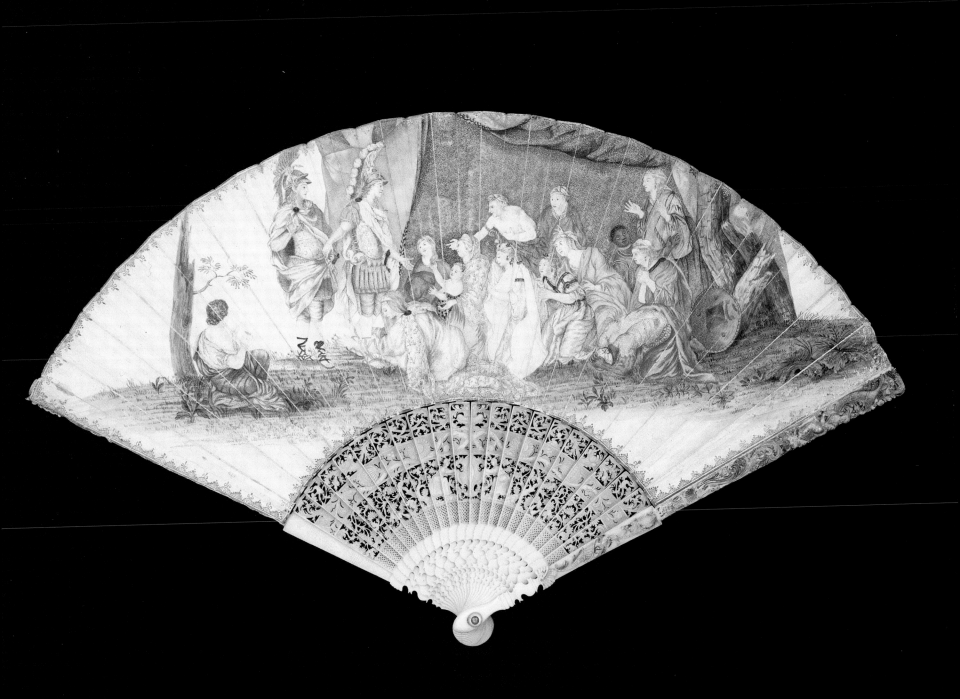

Rinaldo in the Garden of Armida (cat. 8)

Italy (Venice ?), 1730s
Paper leaf (double), painted in gouache
18 ivory sticks with lacquerwork and gilt
Large mother-of-pearl thumbguard (obverse broken) and washer
Guard: 30 cm. Maximum open: 53 cm. Arc: 130° Acc. no. 1976.190

The obverse scene illustrates a passage from Torquato Tasso's *Gerusalemme Liberata* (1581), in which Rinaldo sits in the garden of the enchanting witch Armida. Here the subject is given a cool and dignified treatment. The painting style is sophisticated and personal. Later on, the French painter François Boucher, predictably, would give the scene a different emphasis exploiting the voluptuous potential of the situation by portraying Armida as a being "who incarnates the passion and pleasure that destroy reason."[1]

The subject also inspired several composers. Handel's opera *Rinaldo*, first performed on February 24, 1711, was particularly lavish, with live birds filling Armida's garden.[2] Gluck's *Armide* debuted in 1777.

The fan border merits special attention, with its pink-edged blue-and-white reserves and its alternating bands of red and green gilded designs, interrupted by purple shells at the center. A striking design showing four large standing birds and two others in flight decorates the reverse, surrounded by the same green-and-red border.[3] The sticks are remarkable panels of lacquerwork, surmounted by a shell motif and carved, gilded figures topped by a rosette. Venice had long been noted as a center for "lacquer" manufacture, a technique probably imported from the Near East.

1. Rensselaer W. Lee, "Tasso and Art" (Lecture delivered at Middlebury College, Middlebury, Vt., January 15, 1970).

2. See George Woolliscroft Rhead, *History of the Fan* (Philadelphia, 1910), p. 166 and ill. facing p. 1.

3. For border comparisons, see *The Accusation of Tuccia* (cat. no. 4) and Nancy Armstrong, *Fans from the Fitzwilliam* (Cambridge, 1985), pl. 10.

Moses Striking the Rock (cat. 9)

England, c. 1740[1]
Skin leaf (single), etched and painted in gouache; applied bits of mother-of-pearl
15 ivory sticks, pierced and painted; one guard and at least 4 inner sticks missing
Large mother-of-pearl washer and brass rivet
Guard: 27.5 cm. Maximum open: 46 cm. Arc: 125° Acc. no. 1976.291

Moses, accompanied by his brother Aaron, stands at top center, wearing a red mantle over a purple robe. Aaron, the high priest, in a turban, ephod (tunic) and breastplate, carries an incense burner. A river gushes from the rock that Moses struck with his rod. Thirsty Israelites and animals drink from the stream. In the left distance, the tents of the Israelites are visible. The tabernacle and the Ark of the Covenant appear at right, guarded by the pillar of cloud by day.[2] Variously shaped bits of mother-of-pearl decorate the trees, plants, and garments, representing the manna sent by God to feed the starving people.

On the sticks, a chinoiserie scene has suffered serious paint loss. Two Oriental figures wear short kimonos, obis, and high-brimmed hats surmounted by cockades.

A sketchy pastoral scene decorates the reverse.

1. Traces of the publisher's inscription (in English) are visible on the leaf. The subject was published by M. Gamble "according to the late Act, 1740," "doubtless for church use" (George Woolliscroft Rhead, *History of the Fan* [Philadelphia, 1910], p. 251).

2. The artist has combined imagery from several biblical passages: Exodus 16:14-36 (manna); Exodus 17:1-7 and Numbers 20:8-11 (water from the rock). Psalm 78 also contains references to the manna, water and the pillar of cloud.

Queen Esther
Before King Ahasuerus (cat. 10)

Netherlands(?), 1740s
Skin leaf (double), painted in gouache
20 ivory sticks, pierced and carved; guard deeply carved,
with chinoiserie and ribbon motif
Mother-of-pearl washer at brass rivet
Guard: 29 cm. Maximum open: 52.5 cm. Arc: 140° Acc. no. 1976.352

A central cartouche depicting Esther kneeling before Ahasuerus is placed against a finely striped background of dark and light pink, painted with regularly placed forget-me-nots and a trompe l'oeil design of lace and ribbons. The painted lace coils and twists around the central roundel and is repeated on the guards.[1]

The book of Esther (4:11-5:2) describes the moment depicted on the fan. "All the king's courtiers and the people of the provinces are aware that if any person . . . enters the king's presence in the inner court unbidden, . . . that person shall be put to death, unless the king stretches out to him the golden scepter; then and then only shall he live." To save her people, threatened with extermination, Queen Esther takes that chance. "When the king caught sight of Queen Esther standing in the court, she won his favor and he stretched out to her the golden scepter which he was holding. Thereupon Esther approached and touched the head of the scepter."

The sticks, when opened, form three cartouches. A vase of flowering branches with two exotic birds, a chinoiserie motif, is in the center. A chinoiserie figure also appears on the guards.

1. Painted lace is often found on Flemish and Italian fans. See Susan Mayor, *Collecting Fans* (New York, 1980), pp. 38, 39.

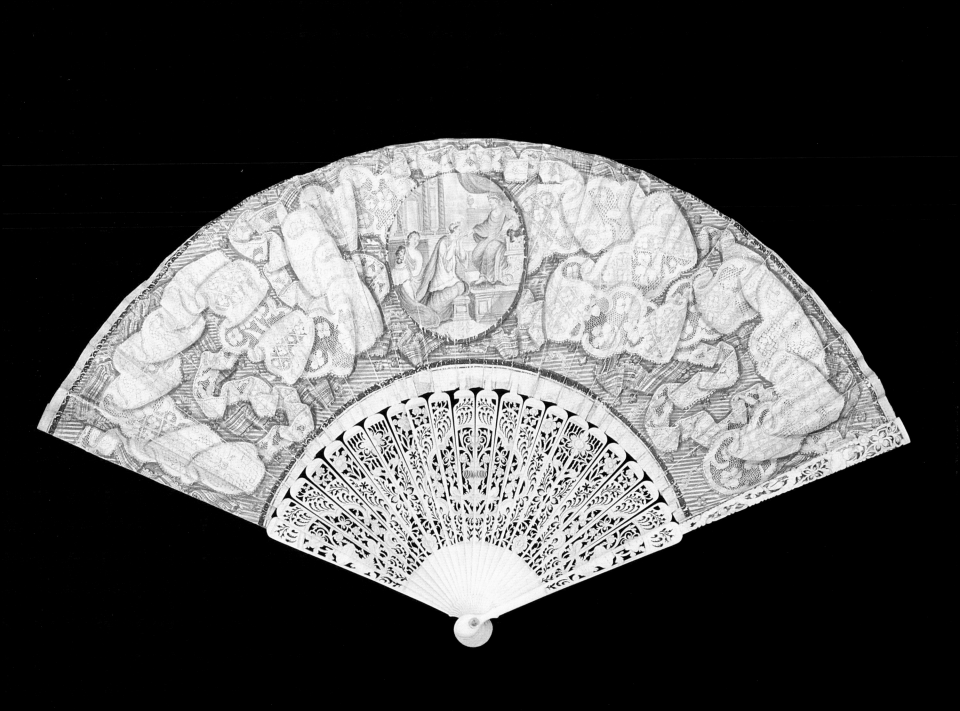

The Death of Sophonisba *(cat. 11)*

Italy, mid-18th century
Skin leaf (double), painted in gouache with touches of gilt
13 faux tortoiseshell sticks, carved and gilded with applied metal
ornament and many diamond paste jewels on guards and at rivet
Guard: 29 cm. Maximum open: 55 cm. Arc: 175° Acc. no. 52.1746
Gift of Miss Pauline Fenno

A seated queen strikes a tragic pose at center, holding a letter in her left hand and a dish of poison, presumably, in her right. She seems to have had a choice, for the servant's tray holds a dagger as well. She is surrounded by attendants, whose gestures express their distress and their devotion to their mistress.

Sophonisba was the daughter of the Carthaginian general Hasdrubal. Her tragedy evolved from the struggle between Carthage and Rome. First betrothed to Masinissa, a Numidian prince, she was married to another prince for political reasons. Masinissa, fighting with the Romans under Scipio, defeated her husband and captured his city. He took Sophonisba away with him, intending to marry her. Scipio, however, feared her pro-Carthaginian influence and ordered Masinissa to surrender her. To save her from captivity, Masinissa sent the poison, which she drank willingly and died.[1]

The melodramatic potential of the story inspired a number of plays, in both France and England. Pierre Corneille wrote *Sophonisbe* in 1663 and was recommended for a pension by Colbert the same year. James Thomson's play on the subject (1730) produced the much-lampooned line, "Oh! Sophonisba, Sophonisba, oh!" parodied by Henry Fielding as "O Huncamunca, Huncamunca, O."

The sticks may be a nineteenth-century replacement. The guards are backed with mica or thin sheets of iridescent mother-of-pearl.

1. See Livy, *Livy*, trans. Frank Gardner Moore, 14 vols. (Cambridge, Mass., 1909), 8: bk. 30, pp. 419-21.

The Story of Joseph (cat. 12)

Netherlands, 1740s
Paper leaf (single), painted in gouache
22 ivory sticks, pierced, carved, painted, and gilded; guard elaborately carved, with broad shoulder, backed with red foil.
Carved head, encircled by serpent, at rivet
In closed position, stick edges form floral design
Guard: 26 cm. Maximum open: 49 cm. Arc: 175° Acc. no. 1976.321

Both leaf and sticks of this large fan are surcharged with decoration. Ornate, garlanded rococo frames divide the leaf into three scenes. These frame dividers widen at the top to enclose small landscape scenes placed almost continuously across the upper edge.

The three main scenes illustrate episodes from the story of Joseph as recounted in Genesis. At left, Joseph tells his brothers that he dreamed that one day they would do him honor. The prophecy is fulfilled in the central scene. His brothers kneel before Joseph, now a ruler in Egypt, who greets his youngest brother, Benjamin, in the presence of his wife, Asenath, and sons, Ephraim and Manasseh. The caravan at far right represents the migration of Jacob and his family to Egypt.[1]

The remarkable sticks are partially painted gray and enlivened with touches of gold. The central scene on the sticks is possibly the Continence of Scipio. Small chinoiserie figures are carved near the guards. The throat area is accented with lacy cutwork, and spaces between the scenes are filled with multicolored floral decoration and designs of gold on white with ink details. On the reverse, nine figures in more or less classical garments relax among classical ruins. The scene is painted over the ribs to conceal them.

1. Taken from Genesis 37:5-11 (the dreams); Genesis 45:1-15 (the reunion of the brothers); Genesis 46:5-7 (the journey of the Israelites to Egypt).

Mercury Slaying Argus *(cat. 13)*

Netherlands(?), c. 1750
Skin leaf (double), painted in dark watercolors,
after Diego Velázquez da Silva
23 ivory sticks, pierced; carved guard
Mother-of-pearl backing guards, diamond paste at rivet
Guard: 29 cm. Maximum open: 52 cm. Arc: 155° Acc. no. 1976.323

The scene depicting Mercury slaying Argus is based on a 1659 painting by Diego Velázquez da Silva (1599-1660), now at the Prado. Argus, the hundred-eyed guardian of the priestess Io, sleeps in the center foreground. Mercury, who is identified by his winged cap in silhouette, aims his sword at the beast. The beautiful Io was the beloved of Jupiter, who metamorphosed her into a white heifer to hide the liaison from his jealous wife, Juno. After insisting that Jupiter give the cow to her, the goddess appointed Argus to watch over the unfortunate Io with his hundred eyes. Jupiter sent Mercury to kill Argus and deliver Io from her captivity. The dogs, not present in Velázquez's painting, are portraits of the hunting dogs of Philip IV of Spain, also painted by Velázquez.

The reverse, which does not seem to fit well, shows an Arabic or Moorish gate, signed by A. Grace(?). It is probably a nineteenth-century replacement.

The sticks are noteworthy. Below the shoulder, the guards are carved into slender colonettes or rods, banded at three places. Sticks of this type, probably Dutch in origin, have been called "pagoda" by George Woolliscroft Rhead and his followers. This seems a misnomer: when closed the sticks form a bundle of rods, recalling the Roman *fasces*, symbols of authority.[1]

1. Such sticks have also been interpreted as "classical" rather than chinoiserie in appearance. See *Fans from the East* (New York, 1978), p. 52, and Armstrong, *The Book of Fans* (Surrey, 1978), p. 27.

Erminia Among the Shepherds (cat. 14)

Italy, 1750s
Skin leaf (double), painted in gouache, stipple technique, after Antonio Guardi[1]
18 ivory sticks, pierced, painted, and lightly gilded
Guard: 28 cm. Maximum open: 54 cm. Arc: 170° Acc. no. 1976.344

Gerusalemme Liberata by Torquato Tasso (1544-1595) appeared in 1581, furnishing artists with picturesque subject matter for the next two centuries. They were inspired by the romantic episodes with which the long epic poem abounds, rather than by its formal theme, the siege and final capture of Jerusalem by Godfrey of Bouillion (or the victory of the church militant over its enemies). Canto 7 tells how the pagan heroine Erminia, dressed in armor, seeks refuge among the shepherds. After it becomes clear that she is no warrior but a young woman in distress, an old shepherd expands on "the advantages of pastoral life over the weary, complex life of court and cities — the old motif of the carefree Golden Age."[2]

Some of this idyllic rusticity carries over into the painting by Antonio Guardi (1698-1760), *Erminia Among the Shepherds*, now at the National Gallery in Washington, D.C.[3] An Italian town and mountainous landscape fill the center background between Erminia and the old shepherd. In order to adjust the original design to the shape of the leaf, the fan painter had to use additional figures. He included a woman spinning wool at the left side and peasant children at the right.

This central scene is superimposed on a purple background covered with wavy gilt lines, interrupted by meandering white lace, which reappears on the inner sticks and on the guards. A feathered gilt border edges the scene.

The reverse, in deeper purple, is painted with a sketchy scene of a ship, cattle, and distant figures, apparently by another hand. Blue and white flowers, a chinoiserie touch, provide lateral decoration.

1. Guardi's painting, *Erminia Tra i Pastori*, is loosely based on a series of engravings after Piazzetta which the fan copies almost exactly. The engravings were published in Venice by Albrizzi in 1745 as part of a deluxe folio edition of the *Gerusalemme Liberata*.

2. Rensselaer W. Lee, "Tasso and Art" (Lecture delivered at Middlebury College, Middlebury, Vt., January 15, 1970).

3. See Antonio Morassi, *Guardi: Antonio e Francesco Guardi* (Venice, 1973 [?]), cat. no. 68, fig. 68.

Provenance: David Belasco

Erminia Finds Tancred (cat. 15)

Italy, 1767
Skin leaf (double), painted in gouache, stipple technique, after Antonio Guardi[1]
10 ivory sticks, painted; pierced guards
Diamond paste at rivet
Guard: 29 cm. Maximum open: 52 cm.   Arc: 140°   Acc. no. 1976.343

Tasso's beautiful pagan Erminia was depicted twice by Antonio Guardi (1698-1760) and is represented twice in the Oldham fan collection (see also cat. no. 14). Guardi's original painting of this episode is now in a private London collection.[2] It illustrates canto 19 of *Gerusalemme Liberata*, in which Erminia discovers Argante dead and Tancred nearly so. Some of the changes made by the fan painter in adapting the design were dictated by the fan's horizontal format; others appear simply a matter of choice.

The central composition remains as it was, with Erminia and Vafrino close together. Width was achieved by moving Argante farther to the left and the Christian hero Tancred right. Rustics and their animals fill the background at left, and an Italian hill town functions similarly at right. Gratuitous changes affect the horse's legs and Tancred's head, and conspicuous writing appears on his shield, "ANDREA BOLOGN – ," possibly the name of the painter.

The reverse is almost more interesting than the front. The leaf is covered with a trompe l'oeil collection of sketch, lace, ribbon, sheet music, portrait medallion, fly, and dedicatory letter.[3] The India ink sketch is painted as if pinned to the leaf and burned in two places. It may be a view of Cesena, a town in northern Italy near the Adriatic, since the name is written near the bottom of the leaf. The background is yellow with blue polka dots. A striped blue ribbon appears to pass under the sketch and over the portrait of an eighteenth-century man in a red coat. A dedicatory letter to a Countess Eleanora[4] is laid on the ribbon under black lace, and a fly walks on it. The lyrics to the music at the upper left corner, dated 1767, concerns the function of a fan and the beauty of nature: "Des zephirs légers couvez troupe enfantine voltigeant dans les airs sur ma belle belle machine belle Machine; Un peintre gracieux de son aimable pinceau a peint ici à vos yeux Ce que nature a de plus a de plus beau de plus beau."[5]

1. Guardi's painting, *Erminia Scopre Argante Morto e Tancredi Ferito*, is loosely based on a series of engravings after Piazzetta which the fan copies almost exactly. The engravings were published in Venice by Albrizzi in 1745 as part of a deluxe folio edition of the *Gerusalemme Liberati*.

2. See Antonio Morassi, *Guardi: Antonio e Francesco Guardi* (Venice, 1973[?]), cat. no. 70, p. 101; tav. 21, fig. 79.

3. Esther Oldham, "Sheer Beauty: Early Lace Fans," *Antiques*, (August 1962): 161-64, ill. p. 163.

4. Born Eleonora de' Bernardini, she married the fourth count of Casteldidone, of the noble Schizzi family. Eleanora, too, was of noble birth, daughter of the count of Massa di Cesena. She was renowned for her cultivation and knowledge of foreign languages. The fact that the verse is in French is a compliment to her skill. See L. Tettoni and F. Saladini, *Raccolta araldica delle armi ed insegne gentilizie delle piu' cospicue e nobili familiglie d'Italia* (Milan, n.d.), vol. 2, "Schizzi."

5. "Hatch a troupe of little light zephyrs flying through the air on my beautiful machine. A gracious painter with his friendly brush has painted here for your eyes all that nature has of the most beautiful."

Publications

Esther Oldham, "Sheer Beauty: Early Lace Fans," *Antiques* (August 1962): 163, ill. (reverse).

Cleopatra's Banquet (cat. 16)

France, 1770
Paper leaf (double), painted in gouache with touches of gilt
12 mother-of-pearl sticks with silver gilt, backed with iridescent mother-of-pearl
Diamond paste studs at rivet
Guard: 28.5 cm. Maximum open: 52 cm. Arc: 170° Acc. no. 1976.224

Surely the ultimate example of conspicuous consumption, Cleopatra's banquet was described by Pliny the Elder.[1] Competing with Mark Antony in extravagance, Cleopatra had wagered that she could spend a certain seemingly impossible sum on one banquet. She is shown here winning the bet by dissolving one of the magnificent pearls from her ears in a cup of vinegar and drinking it.[2]

The very elaborate sticks show a man wearing the fleur-de-lis with a crown nearby, kneeling before a woman also wearing the symbol of France. A *putto* hovers overhead with a crown of flowers and a palm branch. Paired flaming hearts provide additional evidence of a reference to the marriage of Louis XVI, then the dauphin, to Marie Antoinette of Austria. That the fan should celebrate extravagance is a little unplanned irony.

1. See Gaius Plinius Secundus, *Natural History*, 9:63, 119-21.

2. Pliny's editor observed that there was no such vinegar capable of disolving a pearl, and that Cleopatra probably simply swallowed the pearl in the hope of later recovering it. A painting by Francesco Trevisani (1656-1746) at the Galleria Spada in Rome illustrates the same subject with different compositions.

Exhibitions

Fans from the Oldham Collection, Museum of Fine Arts, Boston, November 25, 1977 - March 5, 1978.

Alliance Between Bacchus and Venus (cat. 17)

France, 1765-80
Leaf: skin recto, paper verso, painted in gouache, after Noël-Nicholas Coypel
12 ivory sticks, pierced, carved, and encrusted with silver-gilt; guard backed with gold foil
Diamond paste at rivet
Guard: 28 cm. Maximum open: 48 cm. Arc: 150° Acc. no. 16.307
Bequest of Mrs. Frank T. Dwinnell

In this scene of celebration, the central figures are Venus, goddess of love and beauty, and Bacchus, god of wine. The figures were modeled after a 1726 painting by Noël-Nicholas Coypel (1690-1734).[1] To fill in the width of the leaf, the fan painter gave the deities a landscape setting and attendants. He also veiled their original nudity with light drapery.

The motifs on the sticks show that this fan was intended for a wedding. A man and a woman holding a fan stand before Hymen's altar on which two hearts are burning, while airborne Anteros (Cupid's brother and god of requited love) holds his torch overhead.[2]

1. Now at the Musée d'Art et d'Histoire, Geneva.

2. Family records identify this as the bridal fan of Sarah Meulberry, wed to John Kneeland in 1748. Since the fan appears much later in date, it might be hypothesized that she carried it at her second wedding to the Hon. Samuel Abbott.

Publications
Fan Guild of Boston, *Fan Leaves* (Boston, 1961), pp. ii-6, ill.

Perseus and Andromeda (cat. 18)

England or France, 1780s
White silk leaf (double), painted in gouache after Charles Dominique
Eisen; applied brass sequins
12 ivory sticks, pierced and gilded; guard with heavy top, pierced and
gilded, with plain ivory inserts
Diamond paste at rivet
Guard: 28 cm. Maximum open: 51 cm. Arc: 155° Acc. no. 1976.242

This attractive silk fan is decorated with three oval car-touches, separated by flowering vines and bordered by sequins and a painted bound garland of laurel. In the center, Andromeda gives her hand to Perseus, who has rescued her from a sea-monster. She is bare breasted, crowned with flowers, and dressed in white with a flowing mantle. Perseus wears the winged sandals of Hermes, armor, and a splendid plumed helmet with a golden emblem of the winged horse Pegasus. A classical colonnade and landscape details fill in the background.

The scene is a simplified version of a painting by Charles Dominique Joseph Eisen (1720-1778),[1] engraved by Massard and illustrated in Banier's *Les Metamorphoses d'Ovide* (Paris, 1767), with the inscription, "Persée rend graces aux Dieux de sa victoire et épouse Andromede." The altar, sacrificial animals, and royal figures in attendance in the original have been eliminated. The Pegasus on the helmet was the fan painter's own addition.

The right oval has a circular domed stone monument, the left oval a triangular one. A double row of sequins connected by painted diagonals bands the leaf. The guards are backed by thin mother-of-pearl, or possibly mica.

1. Eisen was drawing master to Madame de Pompadour and a court painter known for delicacy and grace.

Five Scenes *(cat. 19)*

France or Netherlands, 1780s
Skin leaf (single), painted in gouache and gilded
21 ivory sticks, pierced, elaborately carved, and dotted with gilt to
resemble gold piqué work
Mother-of-pearl washer
Guard: 26.5 cm. Maximum open: 51 cm. Arc: 170° Acc. no. 1976.302

On the obverse, five overlapping vignettes depict (*left to right*): children playing; a pastoral couple; a scene from a classical drama; a Teniers-like genre scene of dancing peasants; and two cows in a landscape. The well-painted leaf on its elegant sticks is a summation of favorite contemporary themes. The widely dissimilar subjects are united successfully by the cool green background and by the white grotesque animals, urns, and mummylike figures tucked into every corner.

The central scene may refer to an episode in *Iphigénie en Aulide,* an opera by Cristoph Willibald Gluck (1714-1787), based on a play by Racine. The tense tableau in which a woman confronts soldiers may illustrate Clytemnestra's anger at learning that Agamemnon planned to sacrifice their daughter, Iphigenia, when the Greek ships were becalmed on their way to invade Troy.

On the reverse, a chinoiserie garden scene shows two "Chinese" women with fans among decorative rocks, gnarled trees, and oversize flowers. Three "classical" medallions hang in the interspaces. The chinoiserie is of a type usually associated with the Netherlands.

Beauty Directed by Prudence Rejecting the Solicitations of Folly *(cat. 20)*

England(?), c. 1783
Paper leaf (single), painted in watercolor after Angelica Kauffmann; lightly gilded with applied mother-of-pearl
20 mother-of-pearl sticks, pierced and incised
Star-shaped enamel studs at rivet
Guard: 28.5 cm.   Maximum open: 53 cm.   Arc: 140°
Acc. no. 1976.306

A large central medallion encloses three figures painted in the light colors and graceful neoclassical style of Angelica Kauffmann (1741-1807). The medallion is set against a central section of gray and silver, with lateral sections of fine grotesque ornament, spiraling ribbonlike bands, and winding garlands of applied mother-of-pearl.

Like the many Kauffmann paintings still in place in their architectural settings by the Adam brothers, the central scene on this fan harmonizes with its surrounding ornament. Kauffmann's painting was engraved by Jean-Marie deLatre in 1783.[1]

The handsome overlapping sticks are incised with a chinoiserie design and a central monogram, "ERM."

1. Kauffmann is further represented in the museum's fan collection by an ivory brisé fan, *Cupid Binding Aglaia to Laurel* (1976.298), and *Cornelia and the Gracchi* after Bartolozzi (45.521).

Scene of Clemency *(cat. 21)*

France, 1800-10
Skin leaf, painted in gouache, lightly gilded and embossed
13 gilded metal openwork sticks
Guard: 20 cm. Maximum open: 38 cm. Arc: 160° Acc. no. 95.859
Gift of Mrs. George W. Wales

A meeting takes place in an open meadow lying between a military encampment and a walled city. A veiled woman kneels in supplication before a warrior in theatrical Roman dress. He extends his hand to her and her companion in a traditional gesture of clemency.

The deep leaf and short sticks are typical of the First Empire style, and the classical costumes worn by the women are quite close to the costumes in fashion during the first decade of the century.

II Chinese Export and Chinoiserie

The necessity of appealing to Western taste shaped both the Chinese export fan and the fan made in Europe with "Chinese" details ("chinoiserie"). Neither group of fans pretended to give an accurate picture of Chinese culture. They were conspirators in an extraordinary folly that was part escapism, part fashion, and a wholly graceful and diverting game.

Chinoiserie themes were handled in the Netherlands with particular success. In a limited number of fans, it was the principal subject of the leaf. The majority, however, show Chinese motifs on the sticks, on the guards, in reserves on the leaf, or on the reverse. Chinoiserie was sometimes applied to purely European forms, like the cabriolet (1976.212, Appendix).

As the European fan industry grew in volume, an important part of the Chinese export trade was supplying the separate sticks. These were usually skillfully carved in ivory and often intended for the English market.

Ivory guard stick, (cat. 26)
China for export, mid-nineteenth century
1976.408

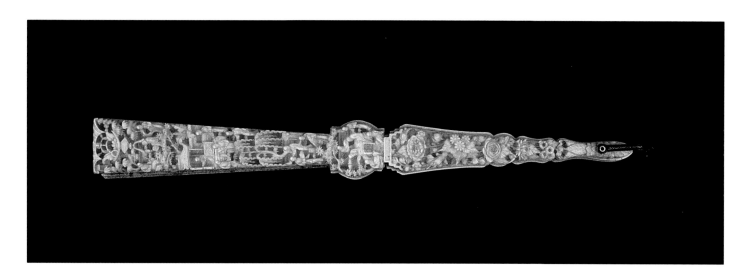

Chinese Imari (cat. 22)

China, Canton (for export), 1700-25
Brisé fan, 20 ivory blades, painted in oil and lacquered
Discontinuous red silk connecting ribbon
Tortoiseshell thumbguards, mother-of-pearl buttons at rivet
Guard: 25.5 cm. Maximum open: 36.5 cm. Arc: 90°
Acc. no. 1976.392

The three figures in the center of the main decorative band are identified as Europeans by their yellow hair and knee breeches, and the rows of buttons outlining their portly figures. An Oriental man approaches from the left, carrying a bundle. Each European has something in hand: a cane, a pipe, a vase. Stylized rocks and red and orange bushes decorate a landscape dotted with gilt. At the sides, long-tailed birds perch among flowers and pomegranates. A lower band continues the motifs from nature, such as flowers, butterflies, and a carp, while the topmost band incorporates gilt swastikas in red frames.

The active cultural and artistic exchange between Japan and China makes definite attribution complicated. In this case, the deciding factor is a striking similarity between the fan decoration and that of a group of Cantonese export porcelain, the so-called Chinese imari ware. This *famille verte* style, which copied Japanese imari ware, was produced in great quantities from 1683 to 1725.[1] Julia

Hutt interprets the fan-maker's adoption of the style as "an attempt to decorate fans for the Western market in styles of decoration which were already familiar and acceptable in another medium."[2] A very similar example is at the Victoria and Albert Museum (Acc. no. 2256-1876) in London. The central scene on that fan differs, however, and a four-petal flower replaces the swastika on the Oldham example.[3]

1. See J. B. da Silva, "Chinese Fans and the Porcelain Trade with the West," *Bulletin of the Fan Circle International* 19 (Autumn 1981): 21-26.

2. Hutt, "Chinese Fans and Fans from China," in *Fans from the East* (London, 1978), p. 30.

3. The Victoria and Albert fan appears on the cover of *Fans from the East* (ibid.). I am grateful to Avril Hart for providing information on the fan.

Exhibitions
Fans from the Oldham Collection, Museum of Fine Arts, Boston, November 25, 1977 - March 5, 1978.

Straw Chinoiserie (cat. 23)

Netherlands, 1750s
Paper leaf (double) with applied dyed straw
15 ivory sticks with applied dyed straw
Tortoiseshell thumbguard, mother-of-pearl washer at brass rivet
Guard: 26.5 cm. Maximum open: 44 cm. Arc: 115°
Acc. no. 1976.183

A sage and attendants appear in a garden of oversized flowers, with a vase of greenery to their left and copper disks scattered around.[1] To create the figures, straw was dyed gold, copper, green, and brown, then applied to the surface. Some of the copper disks are missing and were replaced by mother-of-pearl rounds. The conical hats (one with a feather), parasol, and airy architecture are familiar chinoiserie motifs. Small, irregular perforations, some heart-shaped, lie along the edges of the dark beige leaf and between the ribs.

The sticks are decorated with dyed straw applied to ivory. Flags fly at an entrance gate leading to pavilions on stilts above a curved bridge. On the guard sticks, Chinese figures carrying parasols were given three-dimensional form by applying the straw to an underlying carved ivory model.

1. The crisp, glistening surface of natural straw recommended its use for costume decoration. Examples in the Museum of Fine Arts collection: leather shoes with applied straw design (Europe, 1625-1675, 44.506); bodice, skirt panel, and hat of pink silk taffeta with straw embroidery (France, mid-eighteenth century, 43.1612 a, b, 43.1613); man's at-home cap of blue silk taffeta with straw embroidery (Europe, 1700-1750, 38.1315).

Exhibitions
Fans from the Oldham Collection, Museum of Fine Arts, Boston, November 25, 1977 - March 5, 1978.

Publications
Esther Oldham, "The Fan: A Gentleman's Accessory," *The Connoisseur* (March 1950): 16, ill.

Silver Filigree *(cat. 24)*

China, for export, 1785-1800
Brisé fan, 24 blades of silver-gilt filigree with blue, green, gold, and purple enamel
Red (now rose) connecting (replacement?) ribbon
Guard: 20 cm. Maximum open: 33 cm. Arc: 130° Acc. no. 1976.394

Each silver-gilt blade of this handsome, if impractical, fan is filled with a ground of twisted curls of silver-gilt wire soldered together. The leaf's central band has scrolling floral forms in enamel, a central shield-shaped frame enclosing a landscape in enamel, lateral oval frames enclosing parts of the same landscape scene. The deep blue vitreous glaze in the cloisonné portions may have been made from cobalt, and the green from copper.[1] Individual flowerets decorate the curved tops of the blades.

Filigree was made in many European centers, but the oldest came from China, which continued to export filigree fans from the late eighteenth century until the mid-nineteenth.[2]

1. See George Woolliscroft Rhead, *History of the Fan* (Philadelphia, 1910), p. 56.
2. See Bertha de Vere Green, *A Collector's Guide to Fans over the Ages* (London, 1975), fig. 19 and p. 178; Nancy Armstrong, *The Book of Fans* (Surrey, 1978), p. 27; and Anna Bennett with Ruth Berson, *Fans in Fashion* (San Francisco, 1981), pp. 74 and 120 (no. 38).

T'ang Scholars *(cat. 25)*

China, for export, 1790-early 1800s
Brisé fan, 24 tortoiseshell blades, pierced and carved
Green silk connecting ribbon
Mother-of-pearl washer
Guard: 19 cm. Maximum open: 34.5 cm. Arc: 160° Acc. no. 1976.403

The monogram "HEW" represents the initials of the person who commissioned the fan. The medallion on which it is inscribed is surrounded by figures engaged in dignified activity, such as playing chess, practicing calligraphy, reading, and making music. The smaller figures of servants circulate among these peaceful scholars, carrying trays of refreshment. Above the connecting ribbon, the blades end in serrated curves, each one framing a figure in a different position. These may represent the Taoist Immortals.

The figures stand out against the finely ribbed ground. The natural variation of color in the shell creates a play of light and shadow, like sunlight in a forest.

Exhibitions

Fans from the Oldham Collection, Museum of Fine Arts, Boston, November 25, 1977 - March 5, 1978.

Court Scene (cat. 26)

China, for export, 1850-1900
Paper leaf (double), painted in gouache, with applied ivory and silk
14 sticks of various materials, pierced, carved, and enameled; guards of gilt-silver filigree
Guard: 29 cm. Maximum open: 53.5 cm. Arc: 155° Acc. no. 1976.409

In an airy hall, a high official and his entourage watch a fantastically costumed professional entertainer. The dancer wears a bird-of-paradise headdress with plumes four or five feet long. In the Peking opera, this signifies a non-Chinese character, possibly a prince from another country.

The faces are painted on applied ovals of ivory. The courtiers' robes are actual fabric applied to the leaf, many of them overpainted with blue dots. Royal blue and bright green predominate.

The application of various materials such as silk and ivory to the fan leaf and their integration into the painted design follow an earlier tradition (cat. no. 23). Julia Hutt has related the type to the bone-and-feather pictures of the Ch'ien Lung period (1736-1795) and to developments in lacquer furniture decoration.[1]

The theatricality established in the leaf carries over to the sticks, which are made of contrasting and exotic materials. The guards are gilt-silver filigree, the inner sticks pierced and carved ivory, sandalwood, tortoiseshell, painted ivory, incised mother-of-pearl, and gilt-silver filigree with blue-green cloisonné. A silk cord with a double tassel depends from the brass loop at the rivet.

1. See Hutt, *Fans from the East* (London, 1978), p. 33, n. 18.

Exhibitions
Fans from the Oldham Collection, Museum of Fine Arts, Boston, November 25, 1977 - March 5, 1978.

III Historical and Commemorative Fans

Fans have recorded single, joyous events and multiple, cumulative disasters. In some cases they have served as eulogy, in others as protest. Caricature was an inevitable feature of those fans with a political message.

The majority of commemorative fans were produced at the time of the event they illustrate. Others were markedly retrospective, designed after the intervening years had altered the perspective.

Stamped brass guard stick, (Appendix)
Cuba, 1865
1976.387

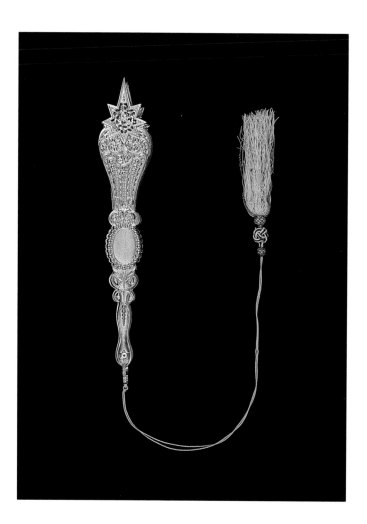

Robert Walpole's Excise Tax (cat. 27)

England, 1738
Skin leaf (single), etched and painted in gouache
18 wavy bone sticks; guards incised with wavy lines, ending in serrated point
Large mother-of-pearl washer at brass rivet
Guard: 26 cm. Maximum open: 44 cm. Arc: 120° Acc. no. 1976.294

Commemorative fans did not always imply celebration. This example illustrates one of the vicious attacks on Sir Robert Walpole, England's first true prime minister (1721-42). Walpole's policy of sound domestic finance and freedom from foreign wars resulted in many years of peace, but his popularity faltered in 1733 when he tried to avert smuggling and fraud by taxing tobacco and wine when they were removed from warehouses for sale. Violent opposition to the tax increased with the Gin Act (1736) and subsequent remedial measures. He was taunted about Spain's claims to America and the searching of vessels. Walpole and the Whigs were defeated in 1741. Created First Earl of Orford in 1742, Walpole died in 1745.

From a reviewing stand, the figures identified as America, Africa, Asia, and Europe survey a symbolic procession moving from right to left. Two people in a royal chariot are pulled by a fox, wolf, bear, elephant, and boar, and equally unusual riders. A monkey in a tiara watches from a pole and two men and a lion follow the company. The lion is labeled "Whelped in the Tower of London." Walpole was, in fact, imprisoned briefly in the Tower (1712), which became a Whig rendezvous point. A rearing horse nearby has just thrown his rider, "K. Theodore ye I." Allusions to Gibraltar, Fort Mahon, and Georgia refer to other unpopular issues of the day. Shadowy ships lying at anchor suggest the effect on commerce of the excise tax of 1733, which precipitated Walpole's downfall. The publisher's statement was partially lost in cutting the shape for the sticks.[1]

The complex symbolism and satire of this attack would have been understood and relished by contemporaries. Lady Charlotte Schreiber's 1888 fan book showed another version.[2] She quoted Wright's *History of Caricature and Grotesque* on the caricatures of Walpole's time. "It is a rather remarkable characteristic of society at this period, that the ladies took so great an interest in politics, that the caricatures were introduced largely upon fans, as well as upon other objects of an equally personal character." Remarkable, indeed, in view of women's voteless condition.

1. The partial inscription reads "[Published by] C. Mosely Oct. ye 23d 1738 according to the late act."

2. See Schreiber, *Fans and Fan Leaves* (London, 1888); English no. 3.

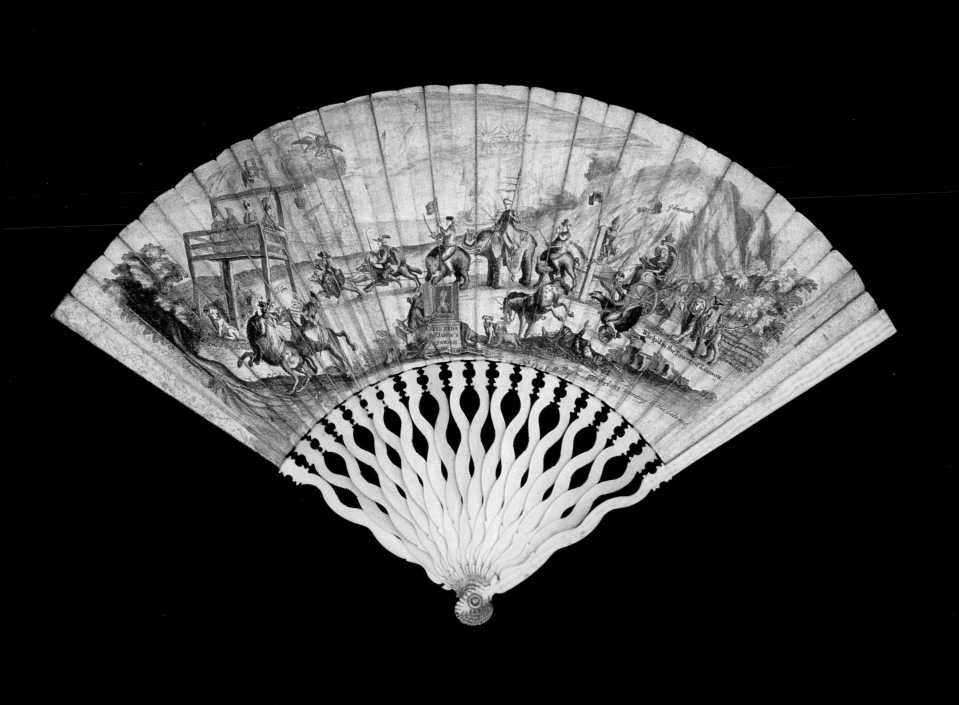

Allegory of Death (cat. 28)

Netherlands(?), 1720s
Skin leaf (single), painted in gouache
22 wavy ivory sticks (one immobilized); guard painted rose, ending in serpent's head, with steel piqué work and etched shields
Large mother-of-pearl washer on reverse and brass rivet
Guard: 27 cm. Maximum open: 48 cm. Arc: 140° Acc. no. 1976.208

A round mausoleum, placed in a cemetery among yew trees, gives off heavy clouds of black smoke from a blazing smokestack and black tapers. Inside, a double-scale robed skeleton personifying Death holds court. He wears the victor's crown, holds an arrow in his right hand for a scepter, a skull in his left for an orb. Black-robed figures circle the mausoleum, some with mourning gestures. Trophies of war lie piled before Death's throne: flags, a drum, an open crown and a closed imperial crown, scepter, shield, skull and bones, and a laurel crown.

Entering from the left are a cripple, a king and queen, and a half-naked prisoner with dangling manacle. Visible in the left foreground are soldiers and a little boy on a hobbyhorse, armed with a stick. A partial skeleton lies in the water nearby. Other figures approach from the right: an old man, widows, and children. A soldier kneels before an empty pedestal or altar. Bones lie scattered on the ground. Overhead are winged creatures of ill omen – an owl, a bat, possibly a raven – flying under a black crescent moon.

Many of the fan's symbolic figures derive from Cesare Ripa's *Iconologia* (1593).[1] Johann Georg Hertel's ten-volume illustrated edition of Ripa's work was published piecemeal between 1732 and 1760. Gottfried Eichler the Younger designed and drew the plates that were engraved by Jeremias Wachsmuth and others. Number 19 in part 1 shows Mors (Death) as a large crowned skeleton lying in an ornate catafalque with blazing lamps. With little alteration, this image translates into the mausoleum of the fan and its incumbent. Eichler's small figure in armor at the feet of Mors appears twice on the fan. The classical armor and the crowns symbolize the power and glory of the world over which Death holds absolute sway.

> Not rank nor dignity can me withstand
> My power extends o'er every land.

1. Cesare Ripa, *Baroque and Rococo Imagery: The 1758-60 Hertel Edition of Ripa's 'Iconologia,'* ed. Edward A. Maser (New York; 1971), xi-xv, part 1, p. 19.

Exhibitions

Fans from the Oldham Collection, Museum of Fine Arts, Boston, November 25, 1977 - March 5, 1978.

Prince Charles James Edward Stuart (cat. 29)

England, 1745
Paper leaf (double), engraved and painted in watercolor after engraving by Sir Robert Strange
19 ivory sticks, carved; guard painted
Mother-of-pearl washer at brass rivet
Guard: 29 cm. Maximum open: 50 cm. Arc: 115° Acc. no. 1976.292

This fan commemorates the second Jacobite rebellion, known as "The '45" and its leader, Prince Charles James Edward Stuart. The Young Pretender to the throne of Great Britain is surrounded by symbolic figures. While Britannia sits grieving at the extreme left, Bonnie Prince Charlie is crowned by Fame, blowing a trumpet above an altar of flaming hearts. Venus, attended by Cupid, points to him as he marches toward the right, dressed in armor and holding a sword. He is supported by Mars and Bellona. Jupiter is shown with his eagle and thunderbolts, scattering the opposition, presumably the Hanoverians. A repellent figure with snakes and torch represents Rapine and Murder, according to Lady Charlotte Schreiber, who published another example of the same engraving by Sir Robert Strange (1721-1795).[1]

The Jacobite rebellion (from the Latin *Jacobus* or James) of 1745 was the last Stuart effort to regain the throne of England.[2] When Queen Anne, mother of seventeen children, died in 1714 without surviving descendants, the crown had passed by act of succession to the Protestant house of Hanover instead of to the Catholic house of Stuart. After some rioting and a brief rebellion, known as "the '15," the Old Pretender, father of Prince Charles, fled to France. In the later uprising, Prince Charles landed in Scotland, entered Edinburgh, and marched down into England as far as Derby. But the Jacobite cause was strong in Scotland only, and the prince met decisive defeat at Culloden. He, too, escaped to France, thanks to the loyalty of Flora MacDonald.

Sir Robert Strange was sympathetic to the Jacobite cause. He joined Prince Charles's party and was named engraver to the prince. Like his patron, he escaped to France after Culloden. Returning to London after the peace, he began a long and successful career there and on the Continent. He has been called "father of that arduous and difficult branch of the art [historical engraving] in this country [England]."[3]

The figures of Mars and Bellona have been identified by George Woolliscroft Rhead and others as Cameron of Lochiel and Flora MacDonald.[4] But the very confident and optimistic mood in which the hero is represented suggests that the engraving was made before his defeat. Flora MacDonald's role followed Culloden, when the prince's hopes were crushed and his life in danger. It seems more reasonable to accept Mars and Bellona as symbolic figures, without a personal identification.

1. See Schreiber, *Fans and Fan Leaves* (London, 1888), English no. 106. The original engraving appeared in Tobias George Smollett's *The Complete History of England* in 16 volumes, published 1758-65.

2. The name Jacobite refers to the adherents of the exiled English king James II and his descendants.

3. *Bryan's Dictionary of Painters and Engravers*, vol. V, (London, 1919), p. 135.

4. See George Woolliscroft Rhead, *History of the Fan* (Philadelphia, 1910), pp. 243-44.

The Treaty of Teschen (cat. 30)

France(?), for the German market, 1779
Silk leaf (single), painted in gouache; applied brass sequins
12 ivory sticks, pierced and gilded
Guard: 28.5 cm. Maximum open: 53 cm. Arc: 150° Acc. no. 1976.236

The Treaty of Teschen in 1779 ended the War of the Bavarian Succession and established Frederick the Great's supremacy. This fan leaf celebrates the truce. The goddess Minerva in pink tunic and plumed helmet stands at center with shield on arm and spear in hand. A young tree, presumably an olive, grows at left. Symbolic objects litter the ground: globe, sickle, lute, and book. Two medallion portraits hang by ribbons from the sequined border. They represent the two adversaries, Emperor Joseph II of Austria and King Frederick of Prussia, who did, indeed, stare at each other across the River Elbe in the campaign of 1778. Sequins enclose the medallions in scallops and form an irregular frame uniting the portraits with two lateral vignettes.

The identity of the principals is not in doubt. The aging Frederick the Great, typically hunched forward and wear-ing his Order of the Black Eagle, is unmistakable. The comparatively young Joseph II is known through portraits. In 1779 he was still co-regent of Austria with his mother, Maria Theresa, shown at lower right, pointing to her crown as she does in her official poses. The personage at lower left is less certain. He wears the high boots of the Prussian soldier, a rather fanciful pink tunic, red coat, and a short blue cape trimmed with ermine. He is probably Prince Henry of Prussia, brother to Frederick, famous for his military exploits and prominent in the Bavarian war. He stands before a dark battle scene.

Publications

Celebration of Esther Oldham: A Tribute to a Beloved Patron of Fans, Fan Association of North America (Boston, 1985), p. 5, ill. with caption.

The Alchemist (cat. 31)

France or England, 1780s
Skin leaf (single), printed and painted in watercolor
12 ivory sticks, pierced and painted; guard pierced and painted
Mother-of-pearl washer at rivet
Guard: 28.5 cm. Maximum open: 52 cm. Arc: 140° Acc. no. 1976.185

Alchemy is the pretended art of transmuting base metals into noble ones, specifically gold and silver. The idea can be traced back a thousand years from the Greeks of Alexandria, through Arabic manuscripts, to the Latin translations used in the Middle Ages. The prefix "al-" is a reminder of the Arabic phase of this pseudoscience, which was the chemistry of the Middle Ages. While Paracelsus declared in the early sixteenth century that the preparation of medicines was the true object of alchemy, the hope of finding a way to manufacture gold lingered and was still turning sensible heads well into the eighteenth century. Sir Nathaniel William Wraxall, author of historical memoirs, noted that in Vienna alone there were three thousand persons engaged in the "study" of alchemy in 1779.[1]

The alchemist seated at center mulls over his magical formulae. The sun, moon, and stars overhead indicate the alchemical belief that metals relate to heavenly bodies. The retort on the central furnace produces a shower of coins, which are being collected by a workman. Others apply a bellows (*left*) and deal with a small explosion (*right*). A second alchemist (*right foreground*) points to a more elaborate machine. The aerial visitor may represent King Midas, who turned everything he touched into gold.

1. Wraxall, in Max von Boehn, *Modes and Manners* (London, 1935), vol. 4, p. 90.

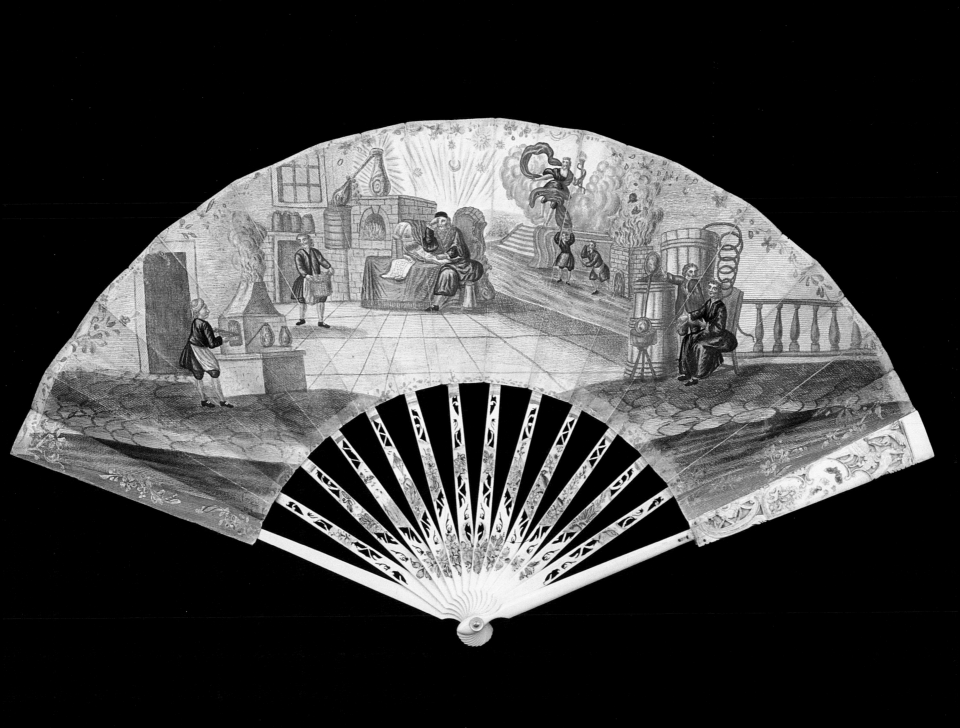

Dogger Bank *(cat. 32)*

Netherlands, 1781
Skin leaf (single), painted in watercolor and gilded
14 ivory sticks, pierced and incised; guard pierced and backed with mica, portrait medallions
Diamond paste studs at rivet
Guard: 27 cm. Maximum open: 51 cm. Arc: 150° Acc. no. 1976.320

The fan commemorates the sea battle of the Dogger Bank, fought in the North Sea on August 5, 1781, between seven English ships under Vice Admiral Hyde Parker against seven Dutch vessels commanded by Admiral Zoutman.[1] Although the battle was indecisive, this fan patriotically presents it as a victory for the Dutch.

The warships, shown exchanging fire, are almost engulfed by the smoke from their cannons. A merman blowing a horn holds up a Dutch flag inscribed with Zoutman's name. The flag of the mermaid opposite, which dips into the water, bears the name of Parker. Below the central scene, the inscription reads:

A[F]BEELDING VAN DEN ZEESLAG IN DE NOORTZEE TUSSEN DE HOLLAN[D]SE EN [DE] ENGELSEVLOOTEN DEN 5 AGUSTUS 1781.[2]

A few flowering vines fill the corners and hang from gilt "hooks" on the narrow gilt border enclosing the leaf. The sticks have a conventional design of birds and flowers.

Reporting on fan sales in the *Bulletin* of the Fan Circle International for Winter 1985 (vol. 31), the Honorable Christopher Lennox-Boyd remarked on the Dogger Bank fan, "It must have been a common fan, for so many to have survived." Three Dogger Bank fans had sold in the preceding five months.

1. The fan known as *Battle of the Saints* (1976.314, Appendix) commemorates another naval hero, "the immortal Rodney," Admiral George Brydges Rodney (1718-1792).

2. "The illustration of the sea battle in the North Sea between the Dutch and English fleets 5 August 1781." Slight errors in the inscription, perhaps due to inattention on the part of the artist, have been corrected within the brackets.

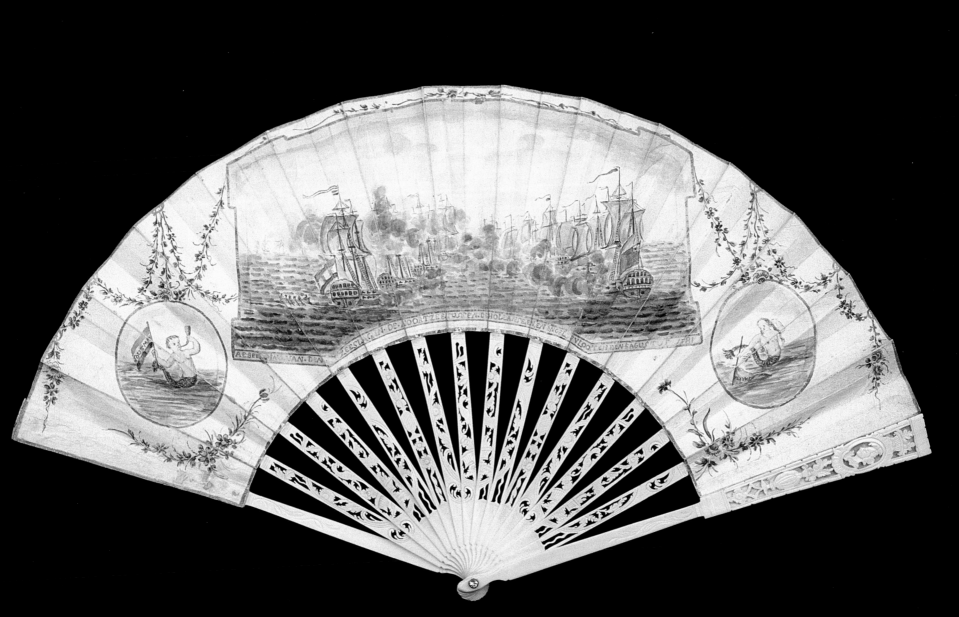

Mr. Biaggini's Grand Air Balloon (cat. 33)

England, 1783
Paper leaf (double), printed and painted in watercolor
16 bone sticks with residual paint and gilt (1750s)
Guard: 29 cm. Maximum open: 46 cm. Arc: 115° Acc. no. 1976.293

Credit for the first balloon experiment in England generally is given to Count Francesco Zambeccari, and many accounts fail to mention his collaborator, Michel Biaggini. A trial balloon was launched from Biaggini's house in Cheapside on November 4, 1783. This "aerostatic globe," five feet in diameter, was followed by a second twice as large, launched at a public demonstration. Three-quarters inflated with hydrogen, it rose from the Artillery Grounds, Moorfields, on November 25, 1783, before a spellbound audience.[1] After two and a half hours, it descended forty-eight miles away in Sussex.

The public experiment of November 25 is probably the subject of the fan leaf, although it does not take place on the Artillery Grounds in Moorfields. Rather, an engraving of the Hampstead country home of Mr. Thomas Osborne, made in 1754, was modified and reprinted to commemorate the event.[2] Buildings and sections of wall were removed from the original engraving, as was a large canopy, to make room for the launching pad. The men were all given large black hats and a parasol was added, but the updating ended there. The ladies wear the large panniers of the 1750s, a style used only for formal court functions in the 1780s. Biaggini's name is inscribed in the cleared area, and his balloon soars in the sky.

Biaggini also appears in a fan illustrated by Lady Charlotte Schreiber in 1888, showing three balloon scenes.[3] He is in the left vignette, where he seems to be explaining his balloon. The central scene depicts the balloon of J.A.C. Charles and the brothers Robert which landed at Gonesse on August 27, 1783, after a forty-five minute, fifteen mile flight from the Champs de Mars.[4] On the right, peasants cautiously approach the grounded balloon, armed with stick and pitchfork with which to kill the beast.

1. A ticket signed "Michl Biaggini Novb 19th" for admittance on February 6 to the Aerostatic Globe is preserved in the Banks collection, Print Department, British Museum (Acc. no. C. 2-20). This ticket may have admitted the bearer to the Lyceum, the Strand, where the balloon was on exhibit prior to its public launching.

2. Lady Charlotte Schreiber, *Fans and Fan Leaves* (London, 1888), English no. 124 (reverse of no. 123), shows the original engraving of 1754, also illustrated in George Woolliscroft Rhead, *A History of the Fan* (Philadelphia, 1910), p. 252.

3. See Schreiber, *Fans and Fan Leaves*, English no. 127.

4. See cat. no. 39 for more on J.A.C. Charles.

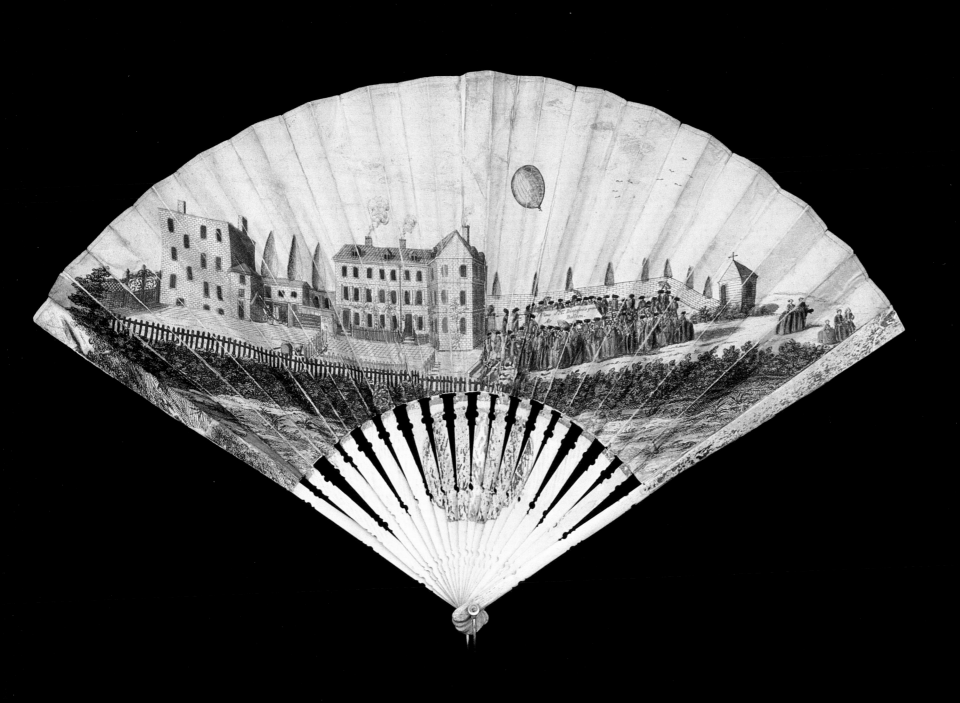

The Recovery of George III *(cat. 34)*

England, 1789
Paper leaf (double), painted in gouache with touches of applied gold sequins
14 bone sticks, pierced
Mother-of-pearl washer at steel rivet
Guard: 27 cm. Maximum open: 50 cm. Arc: 140° Acc. no. 1976.307

George III (George William Frederick, 1738-1820), grandson of George II, acceded to the throne of England in 1760. He had achieved wide popularity because he was the first English-speaking member of the house of Hanover, led a blameless domestic life, and, in general, championed causes that were popular with the people. For example, the taxing of the American colonies to defray the costs of a European war, so insupportable to the colonists, was viewed with favor by most Englishmen.

As early as 1765, King George showed symptoms of mental illness, but they were successfully concealed. In 1788 the king fell ill again and his insanity was obvious, Dr. Willis was called in. His gentle approach had beneficial results. On April 23, 1789, the king went to St. Paul's to give thanks for his recovery. This simple but elegant fan commemorates the king's recovery in 1789 and marks a high tide of his popularity.[1] Inscribed on the blue-violet border at the top is "Health is restored to One and Happiness to Millions." A closed imperial crown in red and gold surmounts the initials "G.R." (for "George Rex") above a crossed thistle and rose. Blue-violet scrolls on either side together read, "On the King's Happy Recovery."[2]

1. Another fan commemorating George's recovery appears in Lady Charlotte Schreiber, *Fans and Fan Leaves* (London, 1888), English no. 110. A fan with an identical leaf is in the Dorothy Quincy Homestead, Quincy, Mass.

2. The engagement of the Prince of Wales, son and successor of George III, was celebrated on a fan in the collection (1976.310, Appendix). Another royal English wedding inspired a commemorative fan in 1981: the last gift of Esther Oldham (1982.451, Appendix) commemorates the marriage of Charles, Prince of Wales, to Lady Diana Spencer.

Louis XVI and Monsieur Necker (cat. 35)

France, 1788-89
Brisé fan, 28 light wood blades, pierced, with applied printed medallions and minimal painting
Red and white connecting ribbon
Long ivory thumbguard, mother-of-pearl washer at rivet
Guard: 28 cm. Maximum open: 45.5 cm. Arc: 130° Acc. no. 1976.233

Jacques Necker, director-general of finance under Louis XVI, reached a peak of popularity in early 1789 when he proposed reforms to extricate the country from its desperate financial difficulties. But Necker acted less the statesman and economist than the banker that he was and proved unequal to the complex problems before him. Since he had advised summoning the States-General, called for double representation for the Third Estate, and permitted the orders to deliberate and vote in common, Louis XVI considered him responsible for the revolution and he was ordered to leave France on July 11. The public outcry was great and his dismissal brought about the tak-

ing of the Bastille. He was recalled, but, unable to work with Mirabeau or Lafayette, he resigned in 1790.

On the fan leaf medallion, portraits of the king (*left*) and his minister (*right*) flank a central allegorical image in which the Common Man bends under the burden of taxation. Like Atlas, he carries the world on his back, specifically the French world, as indicated by the gold fleurs-de-lis.[1] On either side are personifications of the military and the clergy. On the reverse of the right guard is a signature: "Gaahich"(?).

1. See Lionel Cust, *Catalogue of the Collection of Fans and Fan Leaves* (London, 1893), p. 19.

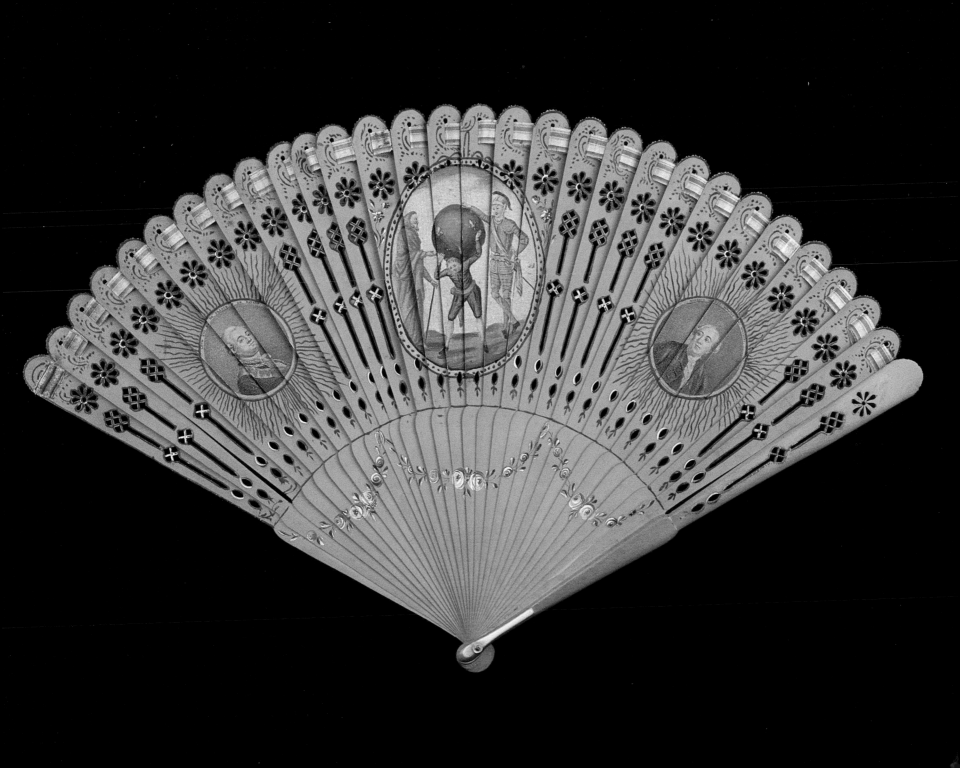

Assignats (cat. 36)

France, c. 1792
Paper leaf (double), printed and painted in watercolor
17 wood sticks; polished guard
Guard: 24.5 cm. Maximum open: 42 cm. Arc: 140° Acc. no. 1976.237

Although France was far better off in 1789 than many other European countries, the government was on the brink of bankruptcy. Coin was scarce, taxes unproductive. Church property had been confiscated that year, and these properties, added to the seized crown lands, were perceived as a solution to the financial crisis. Mirabeau strongly advocated the issuing of paper money, which was to serve as mortgage bonds on national lands. The certificates (*assignats*) represented land *assigned* to the holder, who might (theoretically) demand face value for his paper money if he did not wish to purchase land. In the beginning, their value was undoubted. Mirabeau declared, "They represent . . . the most secure of all possessions, the soil on which we tread."[1] The *assignats* originally bore 5 percent interest, then 3 percent, finally none. Limitations on the number printed were extended and finally ignored. By 1797 the issues had reached a staggering 45,500,000 francs.

On the fan leaf, overlapping printed *assignats* of various dates and denominations are carelessly strewn over a green ground with fine black lines. Their haphazard arrangement expresses the contempt in which they came to be held. One, dated "3 avril 1792," for 50 francs, appears to bear the image of Louis XVI and the words "Domaines natio[naux]." Others were issued by the "République Française" dated "l'an 4 de la Liberté."

1. *Encyclopaedia Britannica*, 11th ed. s.v. "assignats."

Exhibitions
Fans from the Oldham Collection, Museum of Fine Arts, Boston, November 25, 1977 - March 5, 1978.

The Celebration of Agriculture (cat. 37)

France, 1798
Silk leaf (single), with applied paper, textile découpage, and steel sequins
16 bone sticks with piqué work
Brass rosette studs
Guard: 24 cm. Maximum open: 40 cm. Arc: 120° Acc. no. 1976.238

Cybele, the earth-mother goddess of Phrygia, associated with Ceres, goddess of harvests and productivity, is represented here in a lion-drawn chariot, accompanied by wild attendants, the Corybantes.[1] The fan commemorates a patriotic event called "La Fête de l'Agriculture," which was celebrated by the *département* of the Seine on June 28, 1798 (10 Messidor, year 6, by Directoire reckoning). On that day, a procession marched to a temple erected in honor of Cybele in the square of the Champs-Elysées.[2]

The paper figures of Cybele and her attendants were first printed, then hand colored, cut out, and applied to the silk leaf. Swags of sequins are sewn beneath a green border of textile leaves and painted purple fruit.

1. The lion refers to the mythological story of Atalanta and Hippomenes (or Melanion), an unhappy pair metamorphosed into lions by the goddess to punish them for making love in her sanctuary. Later on, in pity, Cybele attached them to her chariot.

2. See Spire Blondel, *Histoire des éventails* (Paris, 1875), p. 162 and fig. 42. Blondel describes the fête and shows another fan commemorating the celebration.

The Christening
of the Prince Imperial *(cat. 38)*

France, 1856
Brisé type, 17 feather-shaped blades of white moiré silk, lithographed and overpainted in gouache with touches of gilt and topped
with marabou feathers
17 overlapping mother-of-pearl blades, pierced and carved, central
cartouche backed with iridescent mother-of-pearl
Mother-of-pearl button at rivet, elaborate brass ring set with simulated sapphires with dependent blue silk cord and tassel
Guard: 27 cm. Maximum open: 50 cm. Arc: 165° Acc. no. 1976.258

Eugène Louis Jean Joseph Napoleon, only son of Empress
Eugénie and Napoleon III, was born on March 16, 1856,
and christened in the Cathedral of Nôtre Dame on June
14. In an article published by *The Antiques Journal* in
1960, Esther Oldham described the event.[1] The infant's
christening robe, mantle, and headdress were of Alençon
lace. The baby was wrapped in an ermine-lined cloak and
driven to the cathedral in a glass coach once used by
Napoleon Bonaparte. The baptismal ceremonies ended
with the master of ceremonies crying out three times,
"Long live the Prince Imperial." Hundreds of balloons
were released, and fireworks were set off and sugared
almonds scattered. The life that started with such pomp
and celebration ended miserably when the prince was cut
down in an ambush at the age of twenty-three, fighting
with the English expedition against the Zulus in South
Africa.

The fan shows Empress Eugénie, seated in a green
throne chair with gold Napoleonic bees, holding the baby
on her lap while Napoleon III in uniform stands beside
them. They are surrounded in the Winterhalter manner
by a bevy of beautiful ladies in voluminous crinolines.
Oldham identified these as (*left to right*): Mme Bruat, the
countess of Montijo, Eugénie's Spanish mother, and, next
to Napoleon, Mme Bizot and Mme de Brancion. Since her
sources are not given, it must be presumed that the identification was drawn from a written account, for the ladies
all appear to be the same age and all have the same face.
A little nursemaid in a white bonnet kneels in the foreground, and the whole group is enclosed in a scrolling
blue border, with three blades on each side of assorted
flowers.

Fully extended, the discountinous silk blades do not lie
completely flat but are slightly angled, giving a startling
dimension to the billowing hoop skirts. On the mother-of-
pearl blades, a costumed couple with flower baskets
underscores the theme of floral tribute.

1. See Oldham, "A French Christening Fan: The Prince Imperial," *The Antiques Journal* (October 1960): 20-21.

Exhibitions

Fans from the Oldham Collection, Museum of Fine Arts, Boston, November 25,
1977 - March 5, 1978.

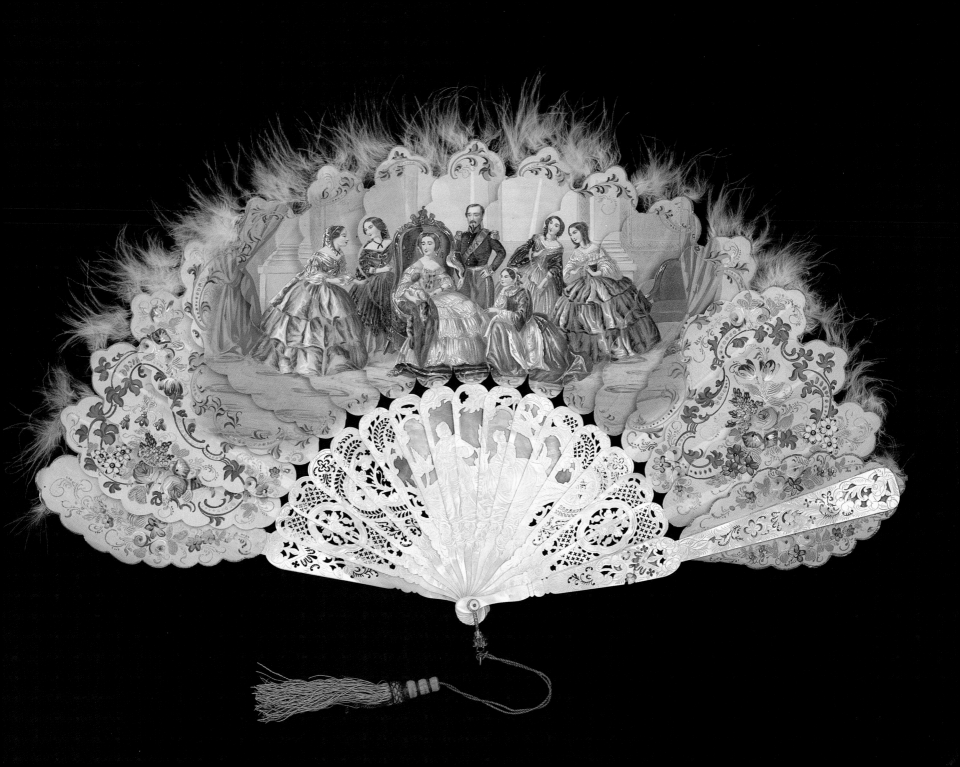

Balloons and Balloonists (cat. 39)

France, c. 1875
Skin leaf (single), painted in gouache, with mica(?) inserts
12 overlapping sticks of reformed protein, painted and partially varnished
Diamond paste stud at rivet, large brass ring
Guard: 26.6 cm. Maximum open: 50.5 cm. Arc: 180°
Acc. no. 43.2078
Elizabeth Day McCormick Collection

A century after the first balloon ascensions, the balloons, their inventors, and the aeronauts were commemorated in this innovative fan. Medallion portraits of some of the famous balloon pioneers decorate the guards and surmount the panels, dividing the leaf into three vignettes. Two additional portraits appear on the sticks, on either side of a ballooning cartouche. The miniatures represent (*above*): Guyton de Morveau, Joseph Michel Montgolfier, the Marquis d'Arlandes, and Jacques Etienne Montgolfier;[1] and (*below*) Jean Pierre Blanchard and Jean François Pilâtre de Rozier.

Unmistakable in the central position is the showy balloon of Joseph Montgolfier, gaudily painted and bearing the double L's of Louis XVI, which rose at Versailles on September 19, 1783, before the king, queen, court, and a vast crowd of onlookers. It reached an altitude of fifteen hundred feet, stayed aloft for eight minutes, and traveled two miles. Its passengers, a sheep, a cock, and a duck – the first aerial voyagers – suffered no ill effects from their adventures. The left-hand vignette may represent the hydrogen balloon ascension of the physicist J. A. C. Charles and one of the brothers Robert, launched from the Tuileries on December 1, 1783. The car is suspended from a hoop encircling the balloon and a net covering its upper hemisphere, distinctive features developed by Charles. It reached an altitude of two thousand feet, was airborne for two hours, and descended at Nesle, twenty-seven miles distant.

These pioneer flights were lonely adventures, but the artist has filled the sky with aerial company. Some of these may refer to specific famous balloons. For example, the striped balloon in the right-hand vignette incorporates some of the features of the great Nassau Balloon of 1836, which traveled five hundred miles in eighteen hours from Vauxhall Gardens, London, to Weilburg, Duchy of Nassau, carrying its owner, Charles Green, and two others. Other balloons with recognizable features may recall the famous ship of Vincent Lunardi launched on September 15, 1784, equipped with oars, or that of Jean Pierre Blanchard (1753-1809) which had wings attached. Blanchard and an American physician, Dr. J. Jeffries, crossed from Dover to France on January 7, 1785, landing in a forest eleven miles inland from Calais.

On October 15, 1783, Jean François Pilâtre de Rozier (1756-1785) and the Marquis d'Arlandes made what must have been the most thrilling flight of all. In their trip in a fireballoon over the city of Paris, they rose to three thousand feet from the Château de la Muette in the Bois de Boulogne, passing over the Invalides, the Ecole Militaire, and the boulevards and landing nine thousand yards from their starting place twenty-five minutes later.

On January 15, 1785, Pilâtre de Rozier, accompanied by P. A. Romain, tried to match Blanchard's feat by crossing the Channel in an east-west direction, starting from Boulogne. His double balloon (gas and fire) burst into flames after half an hour, killing both balloonists. A monument

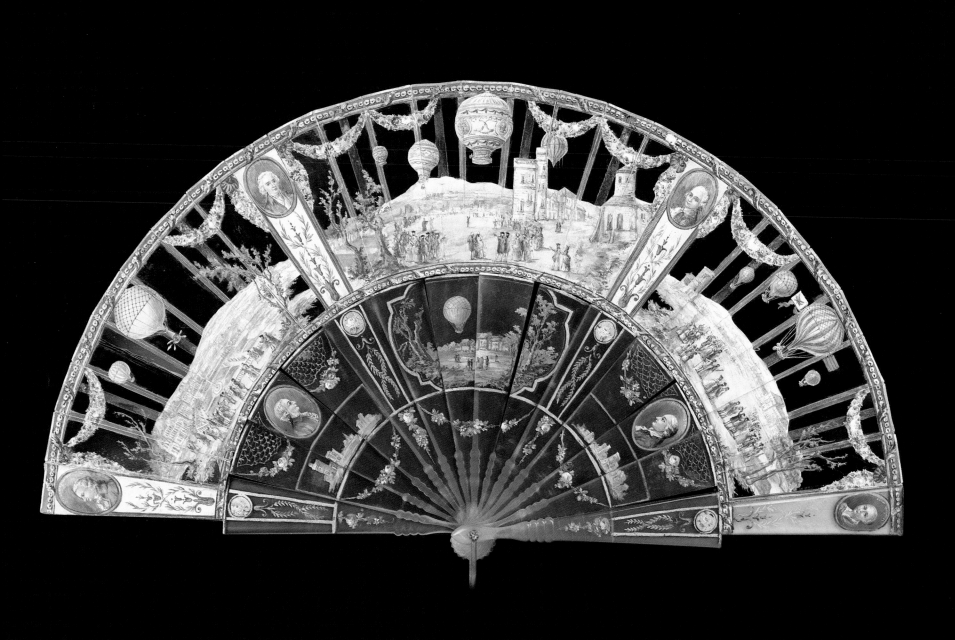

near the seashore marked the place where they came to earth.

The only nonballoonist represented on the fan by a portrait medallion is Guyton de Morveau (1737-1816), a scientist who worked with Lavoisier, Fourcroy, and Berthollet on a dictionary of chemistry. His work with hydrogen probably won him his place on this commemorative fan. De Morveau advocated the use of balloons for military observation.

1. Joseph Michel Montgolfier (1740-1810) and his brother, Jacques Etienne (1745-99), of Annonay, forty miles from Lyon, began experimenting late in 1782. On June 5, 1783, they demonstrated the first practical balloon, made of linen and inflated with hot air. It was airborn for ten minutes, traveled a mile and a half, and started the balloon mania reflected by this fan.

Publications

Fan Guild of Boston, "Continental Fans," in *Fan Leaves* (Boston, 1961), pp. xiv, 2-3, ill.

France, late 19th century
Aqua silk leaf (double), painted in gouache with sequins, signed "F. Creven" in lower right corner of central cartouche; signed "Alexandre" on reverse
16 light reformed protein sticks with piqué work
Diamond paste stud at rivet
Guard: 19.5 cm. Maximum open: 34.5 cm. Arc: 175°
Acc. no. 1976.249

Retrospective both in form and subject matter, this small fan imitates the fans of the First Empire with its silk leaf and painted and spangled decoration.[1] The central vignette, depicting Napoleon standing on a cliff with an attendant holding his horse, is bordered by panels painted with fleurs-de-lis and embroidered with sequins and spangles in star and flower shapes. There are four painted female "cameos." A black medallion in the center of the reverse encloses a gold eagle. It is signed "Alexandre" on the left.

Commemorative fans are usually made to celebrate a contemporary person or event. This memorial, made at least fifty years after Napoleon's death in 1821, expresses the late-nineteenth century's nostalgic attitude toward the past.[2]

1. See Esther Oldham, "Fans of the Napoleonic Era," *Antiques* (January 1970): 135-39, ill. 137.
2. A curious Cuban fan (1976.387, Appendix) commemorates another fallen chief of state: it was made at the time of Abraham Lincoln's assassination.

IV Scenes of Daily Life

Scenes of daily life were rarely represented on fans with any attempt at a realistic portrayal. *Harvesting* (cat. no. 42) comes closest, showing workers in the field. The leisure class with pretensions to fashion was depicted in elegant settings or in fancy clothes. Its representatives were given the props of shepherds and shepherdesses, or even, on occasion, mythological attendants.

After the middle of the century, artists rarely treated the surface as a whole, but broke it up into several framed vignettes. These offered separate glimpses of life as it was or as it should have been.

Ivory guard stick (articulated), (cat. 48)
France, 1760s
1976.186

The Fruit Pickers (cat. 41)

Italy(?), c. 1732; after the painting *La Terre* by Nicholas Lancret, engraved by Charles Nicholas Cochin[1]
Skin leaf (single), painted in gouache in grays, with touches of orange
18 white mother-of-pearl sticks, elaborately pierced and carved; guard deeply carved
Diamond paste studs at rivet
Guard: 29 cm. Maximum open: 48.5 cm. Arc: 130° Acc. no. 1976.220

A garden scene in which young people harvest fruit is painted almost in grisaille, with touches of orange and yellow in the fruit, the faces, and the details of the costumes. The effect is sculptural and suggests an Italian or French origin. The close hairstyle and low oval neckline are typical of the first half of the century. The seated man wears a "pastoral" costume, dressed the part for this idyll of country life as it should be.

The remarkable sticks may be the *poulette*, or Madagascar mother-of-pearl, described by Spire Blondel.[2] Dolphins and seahorses decorate the sticks. On the reverse, the supporting ribs are camouflaged by painted wavy lines, a feature of early eighteenth-century fans. These lines are interrupted by a centered scene of a couple building a house of cards. The man holds a whirligig at which the girl appears about to blow. One senses this may bring down the house of cards.

1. Charles Nicholas Cochin (1688-1754) published this in 1732 after the series *Les Elements* painted by Nicholas Lancret (1660-1743). See George Wildenstein, *Lancret* (Paris, 1924), p. 70, fig. 3.

2. See Blondel, *Histoire des éventails* (Paris, 1875), p. 232. Similar sticks appear in Anna Bennett with Ruth Berson, *Fans in Fashion* (San Francisco, 1981), no. 2.

Provenance: DeWitt Clinton Cohen

Publications
Esther Singleton, "The Fans of the Old Aristocracy," *International Studio* (May 1926): 40, ill.

Harvesting (cat. 42)

Italy or Netherlands, 1740s
Leaf: paper recto, skin verso, painted in gouache
21 ivory sticks, pierced, carved, and painted, inlaid with mother-of-pearl and gilded
Mother-of-pearl thumbguards, brass rivet
Guard: 27 cm. Maximum open: 50 cm. Arc: 155° Acc. no. 1976.341

Under the relentless midday summer sun, two men and two women harvest grain with sickles, while others rest under a tree at left. On the right, a man loads sacks onto a donkey. The composition of the male figure left of center and the position of the female figure in the right foreground were borrowed from Nicolas Poussin (1594-1665), especially the painting called *Summer,* now in the Louvre. With the addition of an authority figure in the foreground, the scene could easily pass for *Ruth and Boaz,* a subject sometimes used for church fans.[1]

The sticks are remarkable for their airy chinoiserie architecture, gleaming with mother-of-pearl, and the shepherd playing his musette in the central cartouche. The guards are similarly decorated with carving, painting, and mother-of-pearl appliqué.

1. Book of Ruth 2: 1-16.

Provenance: DeWitt Clinton Cohen

Publications
Esther Singleton, "The Fans of the Old Aristocracy," *International Studio* (May 1926): 43, ill.

Stagecoach Robbery *(cat. 43)*

Europe, 1740-1880
Brisé fan, 30 ivory blades, painted in oil and varnished
Red-brown painted connecting ribbon
Large thumbguard of tortoiseshell or painted ivory
Guard: 24 cm. Maximum open: 41 cm. Arc: 125° Acc. no. 1976.206

Attacks by highwaymen and stagecoach robberies seem to have been a fact of life in the first half of the eighteenth century. They appear in novels such as Tobias Smollett's *Roderick Random* (1748). Certain costume details, such as the large cuffs and long waistcoats of the men and stockings rolled over the knee-bands, place the event depicted in the 1740s. The guard sticks also are right for that date. However, fans of this type enjoyed a revival of popularity toward the end of the eighteenth century and again about 1880. This example may date from the late-eighteenth or even the late-nineteenth century, possibly incorporating guard sticks of an earlier time.

In the center of this action-packed scene, a young woman in a laced yellow underdress and loose overdress of pale blue is abducted from the coach by a robber. Her companion is drawn toward a cave by another highwayman. In the other coach, a gray-haired man leans out of the window and three women peer anxiously from within. In the lower right corner, a pistol is discharged point blank at a man with a broken sword. His companion lies on the ground.

The sticks show a chinoiserie garden and six small blue-and-white reserves.

Publications

Esther Oldham, "Fans East and West," *Antiques* (February 1948): 127, ill.

The Trinket Seller *(cat. 44)*

France, 1750s
Paper leaf (double), painted in gouache
15 ivory sticks, pierced, painted, and regilded
Diamond paste stud at rivet
Guard: 27 cm. Maximum open: 45 cm. Arc: 120° Acc. no. 1976.226

The scene takes place outside a formal garden landscaped with poplar and topiary plantings. Tall iron gates and servants in evidence carry out the theme of wealth and privilege. A lady in a pink, loosely flowing gown called a *robe volante* holds a closed fan and admires the trinkets presented by a traveling salesman of frivolities such as fans, ribbons, and make-up. Her companion's long waistcoat and full-cut coat with deep cuffs place the scene in the mid-century.

Varying degrees of ornament in the individual dress convey a sense of different social levels: the fashion conscious couple with the salesman, the simpler pair by the sundial, and the serving woman with her wicker basket of cakes.

Delicately painted flowers create a decorative border around the fan. The flowers and their colors are repeated on the carved and painted ivory sticks. Further ornamenting the sticks and guards are representations of hunters, trophies, and ladies seated under garden archways. On the reverse is a loosely painted sketch of a rustic couple by the banks of a river.

120

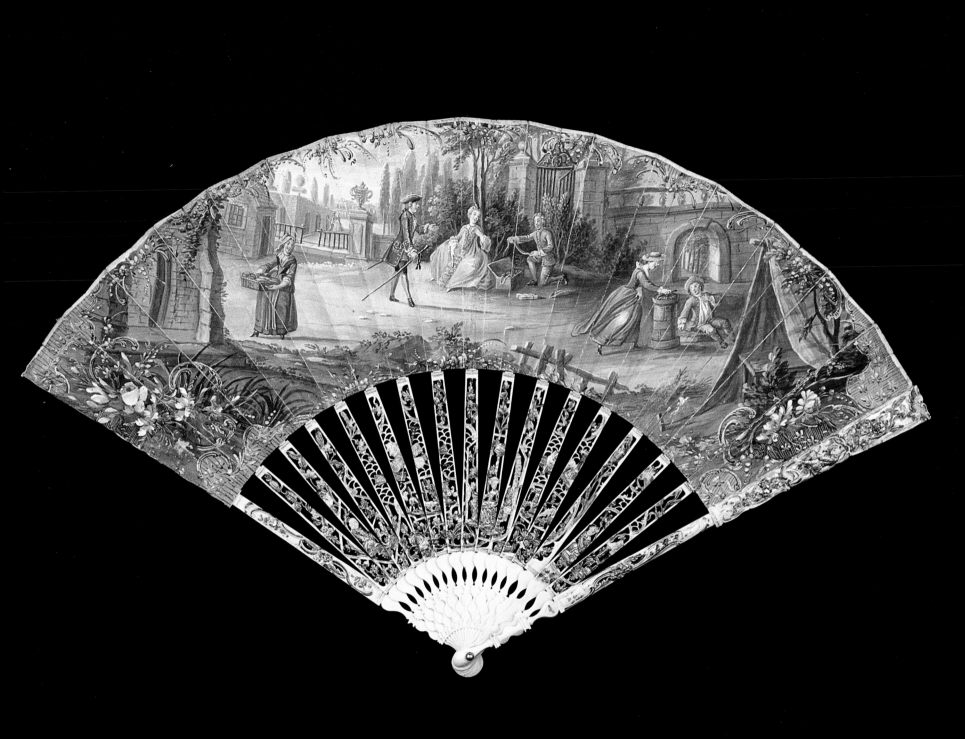

The Tea Party (cat. 45)

England or Netherlands, 1750s
Skin leaf (single), painted in gouache with touches of gilt
22 ivory sticks, pierced, painted, and gilded; guard pierced, carved, and painted
Mother-of-pearl buttons at rivet
Guard: 27.5 cm. Maximum open: 51 cm. Arc: 165° Acc. no. 43.2081
Elizabeth Day McCormick Collection

The leaf, distinguished by its unusual coloration, is divided into five scenes. A monument with an urn occupies the central position, under a blue canopy and surrounded by marble columns. On the extreme left a female figure in grisaille, possibly representing Flora, holds a basket of flowers. Next to her, a tea party is in progress. Two women and a man sit at a tea table set with blue and white china. On the other side of the monument, Venus tries to detain Adonis as Cupid holds his spear, a scene painted in shades of green. Another figure in grisaille fills the right-hand corner; she probably represents a river goddess.

The elaborate sticks have everything in the way of decoration. They are carved to make oval cartouches when opened, with vases, landscapes, birds, and other chinoiserie. Fruit, musical instruments, and flowers are painted and partially varnished on the sticks.

The collection includes another fan leaf with unusual coloration (1976.223, Appendix), painted *en camaïeu*. It shows an English couple before their formal garden.

122

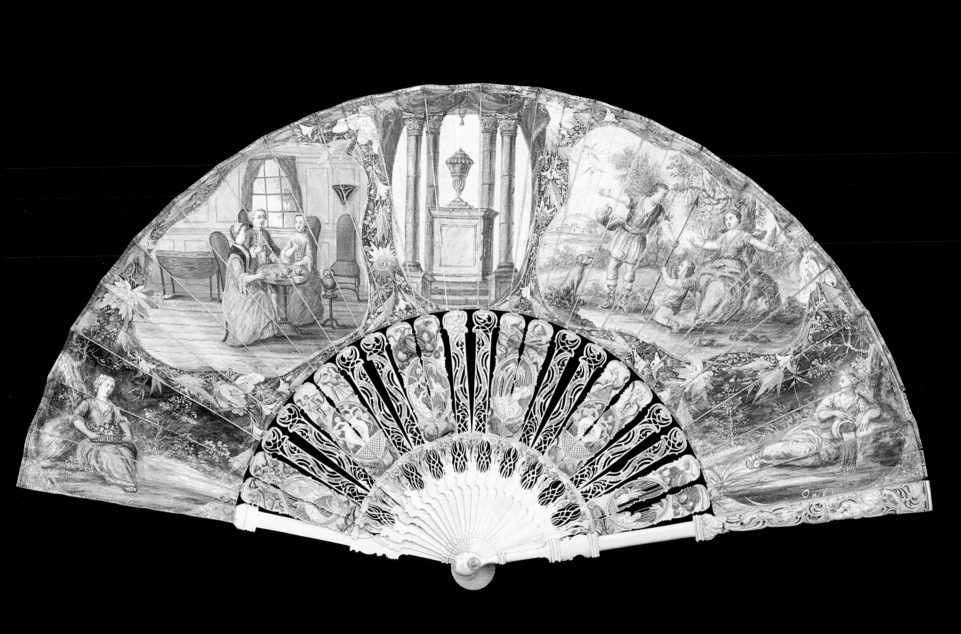

The "Sèvres Group" (cat. 46)

France or England, 1760s
Skin leaf (single), painted in gouache and gilded
20 ivory sticks, pierced and carved with pastoral motifs; applied
mother-of-pearl
Red stone studs at rivet
Guard: 29.3 cm. Maximum open: 54 cm. Arc: 130° Acc. no. 13.586f
Gift of Miss Annie Jewett

The beautiful blue background of this fan, reminiscent of
Sèvres porcelain, is a distinctive feature.[1] The similarity is
enhanced by the gilt border that defines the cartouches
and by the painted and gilded flowers spaced at intervals.
The central cartouche shows two couples in a landscape,
dressed in pastoral costumes. It is a modest version of the
Embarkation for Cythera (see cat. no. 75), with a boat
anchored nearby. The naked *putto* holding a torch is probably intended as Anteros, the brother of Eros, or Cupid,
who represents reciprocated or shared love.

Three figures occupy the central cartouche on the
sticks. The lateral cartouches are filled with musical
instruments, vessels, and martial and decorative objects.
The guards are backed with thin iridescent mother-of-
pearl or mica.
The fan was probably made for a wedding.

1. It is believed that many artists at the Vincennes porcelain factory were also
employed as fan painters.

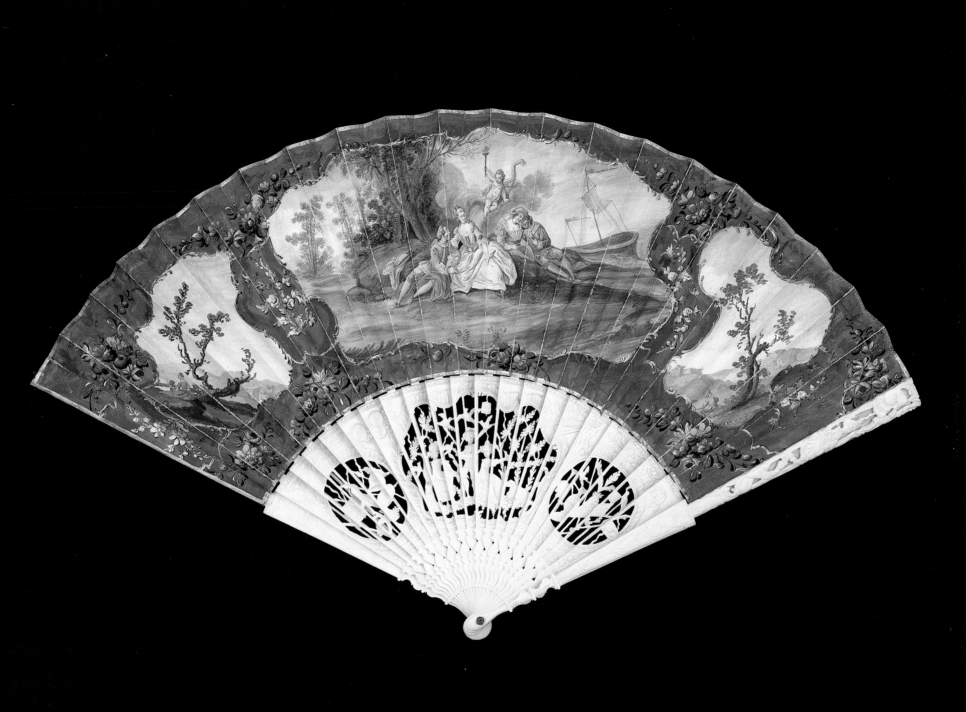

Twelve Episodes (cat. 47)

France(?), 1760s
Leaf: skin recto, paper verso, painted in gouache, gilded
20 mother-of-pearl sticks, pierced, carved, and gilded (one replaced)
Guard: 28.5 cm. Maximum open: 52 cm. Arc: 160° Acc. no. 06.2442
Bequest of Mrs. Martin Brimmer

The twelve storytelling scenes in two registers are separated horizontally by a straight line of painted and gilded flowers and vertically by the same straight-line floral border, radiating spokelike from the shoulder of the sticks to the top edge. The story is not entirely clear from the illustrations, but it has to do with a country girl who is frequently the target of Cupid's arrows and who spends some time in the city, where she is exposed to such seductions as a magic lantern show and, possibly, fireworks. The little scenes are engaging and the painting style consistent. There is evidence that the leaf was remounted and extended, and it has certainly been rebacked.

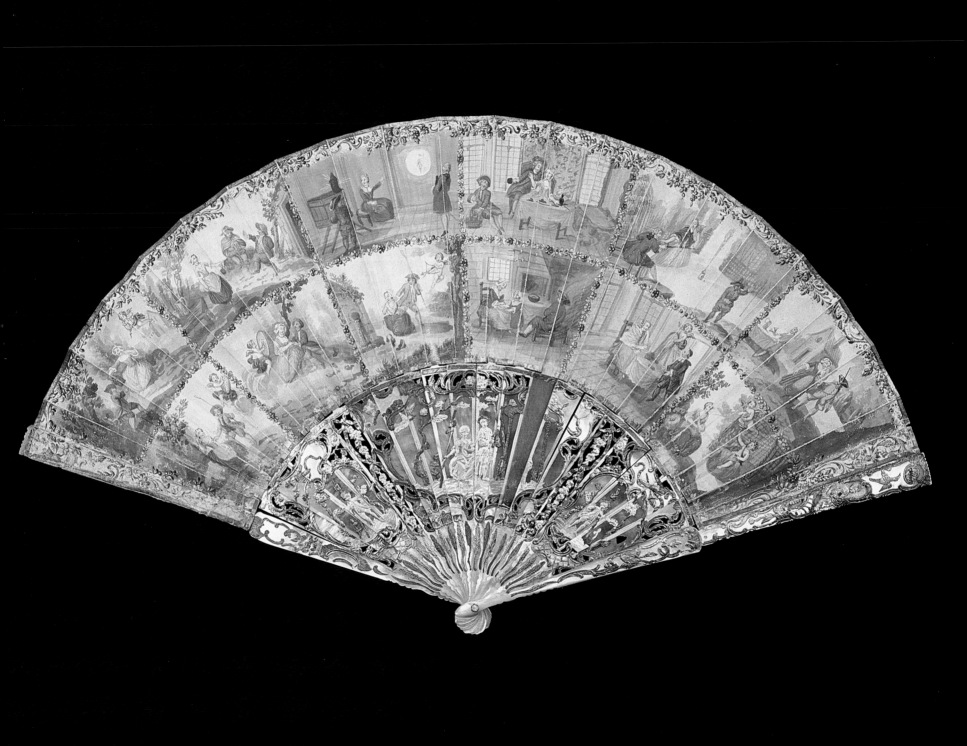

Articulated Pastoral (cat. 48)

France, 1760s
Leaf: skin recto, paper verso, painted in gouache
12 ivory sticks, pierced, carved, painted, and gilded; articulated guards
Guard: 27.5 cm. Maximum open: 52 cm. Arc: 150° Acc. no. 1976.186

A pastoral idyll is enacted before a monument as a "shepherdess" lays aside her *houlette* to crown her "shepherd" with a circlet of roses. A woman holding a brimmed country hat in the right foreground is balanced by a spinner with distaff and whorl at left. A gold border with flower baskets and garlands encloses the scene.

The sticks appear to have been made a little later, for the woman in the central cartouche wears the high hairstyle of the mid to late seventies. Flaming hearts and paired doves carry out a courtship theme.

This skillful but almost routine expression of the pastoral tradition is enlivened by a feature developed in the 1760s. The great Jean François Oeben (d. before 1767), appointed *Ebeniste du Roi*, was also a noted *mécanicien*. His furniture masterpieces often had secret drawers or other moveable parts operated by springs, which delighted his patrons. The fan shows the same interest in gadgetry. In an oval on the obverse guard, a woman holds a gun; on the reverse, a man holds a hunting horn. A slender rod beneath each oval activates the motion: the woman raises her gun to shoot birds, the man raises the horn to his lips.

Exhibitions

Fans from the Oldham Collection, Museum of Fine Arts, Boston, November 25, 1977 - March 5, 1978.

Fishing Scenes (cat. 49)

France, 1760s
Paper leaf (double), painted in gouache, gilded
18 ivory sticks, pierced, painted, and gilded
Diamond paste studs at rivet
Guard: 28 cm. Maximum open: 51 cm. Arc: 145° Acc. no. 1976.217

A central harborside scene and two smaller vignettes on each side are set against a mauve background with a Greek key border in gilt. Three pretty women in pink and lavender seem to discuss the day's catch with two young fishermen at the water's edge. A fisherman can be seen again in the two vignettes to the right, holding a pole and drawing up a trap. These smaller scenes are balanced on the left by vignettes of shepherdesses with *houlettes*. A lonely fisherman sitting patiently with his pole takes up the entire reverse. It should be remembered that fishing was considered one of the fashionable country pleasures. For these handsome, well-dressed people, the activity is clearly recreational.

The ivory sticks repeat the Greek key motif with added chinoiserie details. Gold foil backs the guards.

Country pleasures are the subject of two other fans in the collection (01.6688 and 17.1680, Appendix).

The Dancers (cat. 50)

France, 1770s
White silk leaf (double), backed with gauze, painted in gouache, and embroidered with gilt thread in chainstitch, applied brass sequins
14 ivory sticks, pierced, carved, and encrusted with silver-gilt
Diamond paste studs at rivet
Guard: 26.5 cm. Maximum open: 48 cm. Arc: 145° Acc. no. 01.6693
Bequest of Mrs. Arthur Croft

The two dancers in the center strike a pose for the beginning of the dance. She holds her apron, he his hat, pointing his toe and extending his hand to his partner. Music is indicated by the two players with flute and recorder and by the instruments and sheets of music overhead. The deep rose background is striped with a gilt design and more stripes appear in the architectural setting. Similar stripes appear in the cheaply printed *dominotier* fans which were made by wallpaper manufacturers.[1]

All elements in the design except the figures were outlined in gilt chainstitch, or tambour work.[2]

1. See cat. no. 58.

2. For beautiful examples of tambour work, see Nancy Armstrong, *The Book of Fans* (Surrey, 1978), pp. 22 and 23.

Provenance: Gardner Brewer

A Lady's Occupations *(cat. 51)*

France, 1770s
White silk leaf (double), painted in gouache and decorated with applied sequins and laid gilt-silver threads
14 ivory sticks, pierced, with piqué work and gilt-silver encrustations; shuttle-shaped plaque on obverse right guard
Guard: 27.5 cm. Maximum open: 51 cm. Arc: 160° Acc. no. 1976.215

Three sequin-bordered medallions show a lady's everyday occupations. At left, she encourages her caged songbird to sing by playing a music box for him. Her soft white cotton chemise dress has a matching cap *à la dormeuse*. In the center roundel, she is dressed more formally for her singing lesson. Her rose-colored outer skirt has been pulled up by strings to form the rounded puffs of the polonaise. A tiny cap with blue ribbons and small hanging lappets finishes her soaring hairstyle. At right, she does some kind of needlework. A small pair of eyeglasses rests beside it.

The leaf has a painted brown border hatched with gold and decorated with roses. Sewn and painted ornament fills the spaces between scenes with roses, branches, and charming insects with double striped wings.

The Drawing Lesson (cat. 52)

Italy or England, 1820s
Leaf: paper recto, skin verso, painted in watercolor and partially gilded
18 bone sticks, painted and gilded; guards backed with gilt foil
Mother-of-pearl washer
Guard: 21.5 cm. Maximum open: 40 cm. Arc: 150° Acc. no. 1976.303

In a garden, a boy and girl receive instruction on the sketching of a pineapple plant from their teacher. There are some suggestions that the setting is Italian. One figure sits on a classical relic, and cypress trees, common in Italy, are visible in the background. There was a great botanical garden near Padua, to which this scene might refer.

The top gilt border has hanging fringe, and gilt branches form the side border. The sticks are painted with imitation jasper blue-and-white cameos.

V Découpé, Domino, and Cabriolet

A large folding fan, fully extended, offers the advantage of a screen to shield the feelings or even the identity of the user. The piercing of the fan surface brings ambiguity. Découpage had been practiced in the Orient from an early period, the usual purpose being the creation of a lacelike design. The mask fan, however, with cut out eyes, and the fan with cut out balloons were obviously made with some-thing else in mind. Even the cabriolet fan, with its divided leaf and widely spaced sticks, seems to have had a secondary purpose, allowing its owner to watch unobserved, to spy undetected. (See also 1976.232, 1986.491, Appendix.)

Ivory guard stick, (cat. 54)
England, 1750-60
1976.179

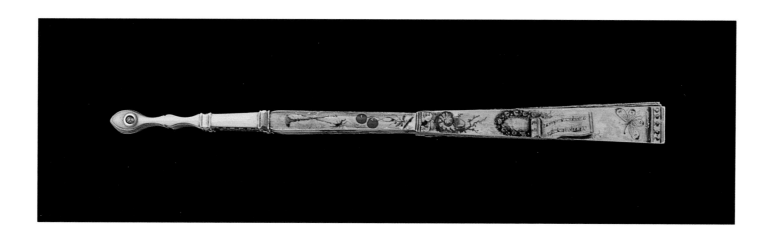

Reticella Découpé *(cat. 53)*

Italy or France, c. 1590
Skin leaf (many layers), cut out with silk inserts
8 ivory sticks
Washer in form of flaming star at iron rivet
Guard: 30 cm. Maximum open: 44 cm. Arc: 110° Acc. no. 1976.182

Examples of lace that closely resemble the fan leaf in design have survived from this early period.[1] While an actual piece of lace may have served as the model, it is more likely that both fan and corresponding laces were based on one of the many pattern books that appeared after 1565. Frederico Vinciolo, a Venetian working in France, wrote the best known of these, *Les Singuliers et nouveaux pourtraicts et ouvrages de lingerie. Servans de patrons à faire toutes sortes de poincts, couppe, lacis et autres.* The fan-maker had to progressively scale down the lace pattern from 3 centimeters (1½ inches) at the top of the leaf to 1 centimeter (⅜ inch) at the lower edge.

Two patterns were used in cutting the nineteen sections for the leaf's outer faces, one based on the half circle, the other on the lozenge. Twelve half-circle sections put together made six rosettes, and these alternate with the lozenges.

The outer faces of the fan establish the principle lines of the design. Another double layer, inserted between the front and back faces, supplies finer fillings and elaborations in the form of triangles, circles, tiny flowers, and serrated edging. These intermediate layers hold bits of colored silk, which gives sparkle and vivacity to the design. Blue-green, orange-red, deep purple or blue and gold can still be distinguished, with an occasional metal thread.

Reticella lace was usually given a finishing edge of points, made in the *punto in aria* technique. The donor stated that the current example had one such point in découpé and vestiges of another, which were subsequently removed. A fan identical in design at the Musée de la

Renaissance in Ecouen, has an intact border of points.[2] Its sticks, which conform to those of the example here as far as they go, lack the final four centimeters (1½ inches) of length. This seems to point to a loss and subsequent reriveting, since the mother-of-pearl button appears to be of a later date than the rivet of the Oldham fan, making the latter more complete in this respect.[3]

1. See Santina M. Levey, *Lace: A History* (London, 1983), no. 36.

2. The Ecouen fan was formerly in the collection of the Musée de Cluny, Paris.

3. See George Woolliscroft Rhead, *History of the Fan* (Philadelphia, 1910), p. 114, ill. after p. 108. Avril Hart of the Victoria and Albert Museum questioned the dating of the Oldham sticks on a visit to the Museum of Fine Arts in 1983. She also had doubts about the lace design. In the absence of a definitive test for dating unpainted material, the dating must rest on the Oldham fan's exact correspondence to the Ecouen example, the date of which, presumably, has not been questioned.

See the introductory essay "Fans as Social History" for background on fans of this type.

Exhibitions
From Fiber to Fine Art, Museum of Fine Arts, Boston, July 30 - September 28, 1980.

Fans from the Oldham Collection, Museum of Fine Arts, Boston, November 25, 1977 - March 5, 1978.

Publications
Nancy Armstrong, *A Collector's History of Fans* (New York, 1974), pp. 21, 22, ill.

Encyclopaedia Britannica, 30th ed., s.v. "fan," plate II, no. 6.

Esther Oldham, "The Fan – A Gentleman's Accessory," *Connoisseur* (March 1950): 14-20, ill. p. 15, no. 4.

——"The Muffs and Fans of the Incredible Dandies," *Spinning Wheel* (April 1973): 20-22, ill. p. 22.

——"An Exhibition of Historic Laces and Jewels," *Needle and Bobbin Club* 9, no. 2, (1924): 10.

Larry Salmon et al., *From Fiber to Fine Arts* (Boston, 1980), 39, ill.

Mask Fan *(cat. 54)*

England, for the Spanish market, 1740s
Paper leaf (double), patched with skin, etched, engraved, and painted in watercolor
18 ivory sticks, pierced, partially painted, varnished, and gilded
Mother-of-pearl buttons on brass rivet
Guard: 26.3 cm. Maximum open: 48.5 cm. Arc: 155°
Acc. no. 1976.179

Four vignettes, enclosed by rococo frames, surround a central ovoid mask with eyeholes. On the far left, three youths examine sheet music and stringed instruments at a high counter in a music shop. Additional instruments hang on the wall. Two folds have been lost at the left edge, eliminating a fourth figure found on related fan leaves.

On the near left is a domestic scene, probably from a contemporary farce, showing an angry woman pursuing a man with a cat-o'-nine-tails. Labeled *"gurumino"* ("hen-pecked"), he holds a mop in one hand while warding off blows with the other. His tormentor's words promise more of the same: *"Este es de dyaris"* ("This is [what to expect] daily.") Ironically, a monkey in the left-hand corner accompanies this domestic comedy on his viola d'amore. A sign overhead translates as, "To Senor Don Mateo Julle, May God preserve you for many years, Seville."

The scene on the near right takes place in a street of three-story buildings, where a news vendor offers *"El Diario de Oy"* ("Today's Diary,") to a woman who has no hand free to accept it. She holds a mask in one hand to shield her face while clutching a conventional fan in the other. The final vignette offers a solution to this dilemma: in a fan shop specializing in fans with built-in masks, like the present example, a woman in red behind the counter holds up a mask fan. Others lie on the counter and hang overhead. Two customers approach, wearing mantillas.

At least six examples of this arresting type of fan have survived in public and private collections from Moscow to San Francisco. They differ in media, choice and arrangement of vignettes, and decoration of their sticks. The printed and hand-colored examples, like the Oldham fan, present the greatest conformity.[1] A copy painted in watercolor at the Metropolitan Museum of Art, New York, has the two lower vignettes in reversed position, as does a painted(?) version now at the Armoury in the Kremlin.[2] The Russian fan links the aforementioned fans to another example, at the Fine Arts Museums of San Francisco, which shows scenes of country life and an urban scene of a lady being carried in a sedan chair. This sedan chair vignette also appears on the Russian fan.[3]

An English provenance for both printed and painted versions is supported by another English fan in the Oldham collection (46.318, Appendix). The sticks of this fan are decorated with unusual motifs, such as chambered nautilus shells, ruined antique columns, and wreaths, all of which appear on the sticks of the Oldham mask fan.

1. Another printed example (formerly Pabst/Baldwin collection) appears in the Christie's catalogue, May 4, 1978, no. 18; and in Susan Mayor, *Collecting Fans* (New York, 1980), p. 53. For another (private collection), see Musée de la Mode et du Costume, *L'Eventail: Miroir de la belle époque* (Paris, 1985), p. 109.

2. In her article "Instruments for Agitating the Air," (*Metropolitan Museum of Art Bulletin* 23, no. 7 [March 1965]: 253), Edith A. Standen refers to the Russian publication *Starye Gody* ("The Old Years") of April 1, 1910, p. 23. The fan illustrated was from the collection of the Countess Chouvaloff. The Russian article attributes the fan to a German source, calling it a *Witz* or "joke" in German.

3. See Anna Bennett with Ruth Berson, *Fans in Fashion* (San Francisco, 1981), p. 36, no. 10, ill. p. 155.

Cabriolet with "Cab" (cat. 55)

Exhibitions

From Fiber to Fine Art, Museum of Fine Arts, Boston, July 30 - September 28, 1980.

Fans from the Oldham Collection, Museum of Fine Arts, Boston, November 25, 1977 - March 5, 1978.

Publications

Bulletin of the Needle and Bobbin Club 10, no. 1 (1926): 30.

Encyclopaedia Britannica, 30th ed., s.v. "fan," fig. 2.

Fan Guild of Boston, "Fans in Opera and the Theatre," *Fan Leaves* (Boston, 1961), pp. 14-15, fig. 11.

Larry Salmon et al., *From Fiber to Fine Art* (Boston, 1980), p. 39, ill.

Edith A. Standen, "Instruments for Agitating the Air," *The Metropolitan Museum of Art Bulletin* 23, no. 7, (March 1965): 253.

Esther Singleton, "Fans of the Old Aristocracy," *International Studio 5* (May 1926), 40, ill.

France or Germany, c. 1755[1]
Paper leaf (double), painted in gouache
18 ivory sticks, pierced, painted, and partially varnished
Guard: 26.5 cm. Maximum open: 45 cm. Arc: 135° Acc. no. 01.6687
Bequest of Mrs. Arthur Croft

The five figures in the upper leaf are engaged in the traditional country pleasures of music-making and dancing. They are dressed in country costumes, except for the lady in the center, who wears a necklace and appears somewhat grander. The obverse lower leaf shows an actual cabriolet, the light, two-wheeled vehicle that started a remarkable fad. Following its introduction by Josiah Childs in 1755, cabriolets appeared everywhere. Walpole wrote, "All we hear from France is that a new madcap reigns there, as strong as that of Patins was. . . . Everything is to be *en cabriolet*; the men paint them on their waistcoats, have them embroidered for clocks to their stockings, and the women . . . are now muffled up in great caps with round sides, in the form of, and scarce less than, the wheels of the chaises."

A single horse pulled the cabriolet, so named for its characteristic erratic movement which recalled a young goat's leap (*capriola*). Concentric bands strengthened its large cartwheels, producing an effect mirrored by the cabriolet fan's narrow, concentric leaves mounted on widely spaced, spokelike sticks.[2]

The two leaves on the reverse show, respectively, a marine scene above, painted straight across the leaf, and a landscape below, with two small figures and some ruins.

The visible portion of the sticks between the obverse leaves and the upper portion of the sticks between the

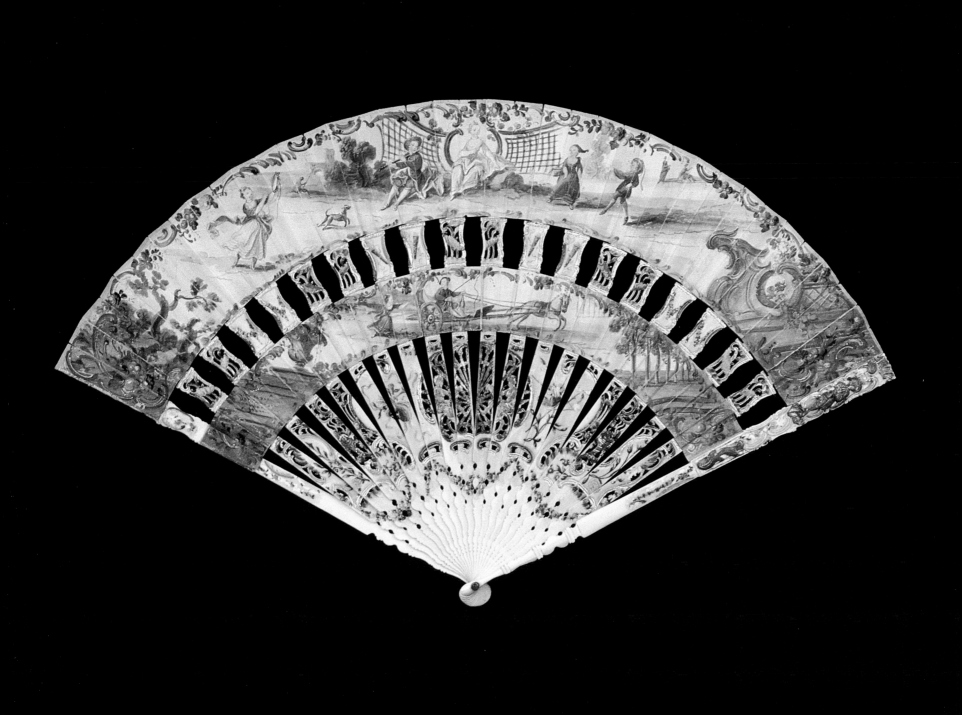

lower leaf and rivet, have apparently been varnished with a material that has darkened with age, producing a spotty appearance that was probably not intended. Garlands, quivers, and musical instruments are the recurrent motifs.

1. The fan was bought in Dresden and belonged to the Gardner Brewer Collection.

2. See "Double Cabriolet" (cat. no. 56), n. 1. Other cabriolet fans in the collection are listed in the Appendix: 1976.211 (in grisaille) and 1976.212 (chinoiserie).

France or England, 1755-60
Three narrow skin leaves (single), mounted concentrically, painted in watercolor
22 ivory sticks, pierced and painted, guards deeply carved
Mother-of-pearl washer at brass rivet
Guard: 25.5 cm. Maximum open: 48.5 cm. Arc: 180°
Acc. no. 1976.210

Within the rare group of split-leaved fans known as "cabriolets," this fan is a double rarity, for the leaf has an extra division.[1] The effect produced is one of lightness and delicacy in spite of the full half-circle spread. The proportions were right for the pannier-supported skirts of the era.[2] In the central cartouche of the outermost leaf, a standing woman wears a rose-colored gown with this extended skirt, a style that disappeared about 1760 except for formal wear.

Other vignettes in variously shaped frames depict harbor scenes, ruins, a pastoral couple, a shell, and a sheep.[3] The interspaces are filled with delicate flowers, insects, and chinoiserie, picked out with touches of ink and gilt. Similar eclectic subject matter characterizes the middle and inner leaves: mostly motifs from nature accented with chinoiserie. Many of the same images are painted on the reverse, disguising the presence of the sticks.

1. See cat. no. 55 entry for description of the cabriolet.

2. Two other cabriolets are illustrated in the Appendix: 1976.211 (grisaille) and 1976.212 (chinoiserie).

3. The subject matter and painting style of the reserves recall decoration on Meissen porcelain of the period.

Provenance: DeWitt Clinton Cohen

Découpé "Cabriolet" *(cat. 57)*

Exhibitions

Dressed and Furnished in Flowers: Fine Textiles of the Western European Eighteenth Century, Museum of Fine Arts, Boston, April 29 - July 28, 1985.

*Fans from the Oldham Collection,*Museum of Fine Arts, Boston, November 25, 1977 - March 5, 1978.

Publications

Nancy Armstrong. *The Book of Fans* (Surrey, 1978), p. 25.

Encyclopaedia Britannica, 30th ed., s.v. "fan," plate I, no. 1.

England(?), 1755-60
Skin leaf (single), découpé and painted in watercolor
20 ivory sticks, pierced, carved, and painted
Diamond paste studs at rivet
Guard: 29 cm. Maximum open: 52 cm. Arc: 135° Acc. no. 1976.221

A "cabriolet" effect, or the illusion of a divided leaf, is achieved convincingly and economically by introducing a lacy découpé section between the painted bands at the top and bottom of the leaf. In the upper band, individual shells are separated by white lace and brown bands with small chinoiserie figures. The lower painted band shows three miniature landscapes.

The banded effect is continued by the treatment of the sticks. Paired pierced sticks with Chinese ladies holding screen fans alternate with other pairs combining chinoiserie figures and motifs with meandering white lace on blue.

Provenance: DeWitt Clinton Cohen

Publications

Esther Oldham, "Sheer Beauty: Early Lace Fans," *Antiques* 82 (1962):   fig. 8.

Oldham, "The Fan: A Gentleman's Accessory," *Connoisseur* (1950), fig. 12, p. 17.

Esther Singleton, "Fans of the Old Aristocracy," *International Studio* 5 (May 1926): 41, fig. 8.

Wallpaper Découpé *(cat.58)*

France, 1770s
Paper leaf (double), painted in watercolor, stenciled, and cut with a stamp
14 paired bone sticks, pierced and painted; guard pierced, carved, backed with red foil
Mother-of-pearl washer
Guard: 27 cm. Maximum open: 47 cm. Arc: 140° Acc. no. 1976.229

Brightly colored block-printed and stenciled papers had been made for more than a century around Rouen, principally for peasants, who bought them to decorate their chimneypieces.[1] Later these papers found a wider market as liners for drawers and chests, as end papers for books, and as cheap wallpaper. The papers, called *dominos*, were about 50 by 30 centimeters. They were first printed from crudely cut blocks of pearwood, then colored by means of a stencil with rather garish colors, which usually included bright orange, black, bright blue, and mauve. The *dominotier* who made these papers was limited by regulations that forbade him to include more than six lines of print in a design, thereby protecting the interests of the book printers.[2]

The popularity of wallpaper fans rose when people – even Royalists – attempted a simpler way of living.[3] These rather crude fans suited the pared-down revolutionary mood. Many fans produced by other methods imitated the domino style.

The present example has the added feature of découpage. Découpé panels alternate with painted and stenciled ones. A metal stamp was used to punch holes into paper to create a lacy pattern.

1. See Jacques Savary des Bruslons, *Dictionnaire universel de commerce* (Copenhagen, 1760), vol. 2, p. 114.

2. *Ibid.*, p. 115.

3. Other *dominotier* fans in the collection: 1976.228, 1976.234, 1976.241, 1976.245, 1976.246 (Appendix) and 1976.389.

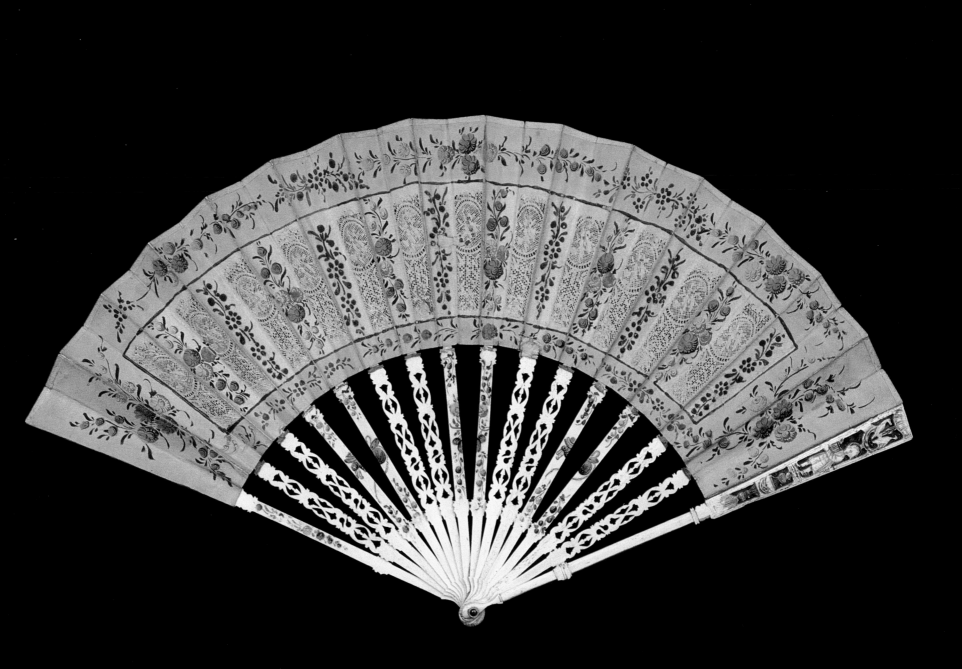

Découpé, Five Vignettes (cat. 59)

France, c. 1760
Paper leaf (double), cut with a stamp to resemble lace, painted in gouache
16 ivory sticks, carved and silvered (now tarnished); guard pierced, backed with red foil
Diamond paste stud at rivet
Guard: 27 cm. Maximum open: 47.5 cm. Arc: 125° Acc. no. 1976.207

The découpé technique used here is unusual in that the leaf was stamped in one piece, rather than in sections to accommodate several sticks only.[1]

The repeating design was planned to show a blossom on every other pleat fold. It is interrupted in five areas by gouache-painted pastoral vignettes, enclosed in gilt frames. The intention seems to have been an imitation of Valenciennes lace with its typical diamond mesh. The découpage is varied to a starlike form in the blossoms, suggesting a lace "filling."

The reserve areas on the reverse side have scenery, but no figures.

1. Avril Hart (Research Assistant, Department of Textile Furnishings and Dress, the Victoria and Albert Museum, London) made this observation, among many others of great interest and value, on a visit to the Museum of Fine Arts, Boston in 1983.

Publications
Esther Oldham, "The Fan – A Gentleman's Accessory," *The Connoisseur* (March 1950): 18, ill.

Textile Découpé *(cat. 60)*

France, 1760s
Silk leaf (double), perforated with a stamp, with reserves painted in gouache
16 ivory sticks, pierced, carved, and painted
Diamond paste stud at rivet
Guard: 27 cm. Maximum open: 49 cm. Arc: 140° Acc. no. 1976.187

In the central vignette, a shepherdess is teased as she rests in a garden, her *houlette* at her feet, by a man who tickles her neck with a straw. Lateral scenes show, at left, a woman with ruins in the distance and, at right, a man playing a large *vielle à roue* (hurdy-gurdy, a "rustic" instrument). Painted flowers are scattered around and between the vignettes.

The silk leaf was pinpricked with a metal stamp to create a lacelike effect.[1] Sticks and guards have chinoiserie decoration.

1. Avril Hart's observation, recorded in notes on her visit to the Museum of Fine Arts, Boston in 1983.

Exhibitions
Fans from the Oldham Collection, Museum of Fine Arts, Boston, November 25, 1977 - March 5, 1978.

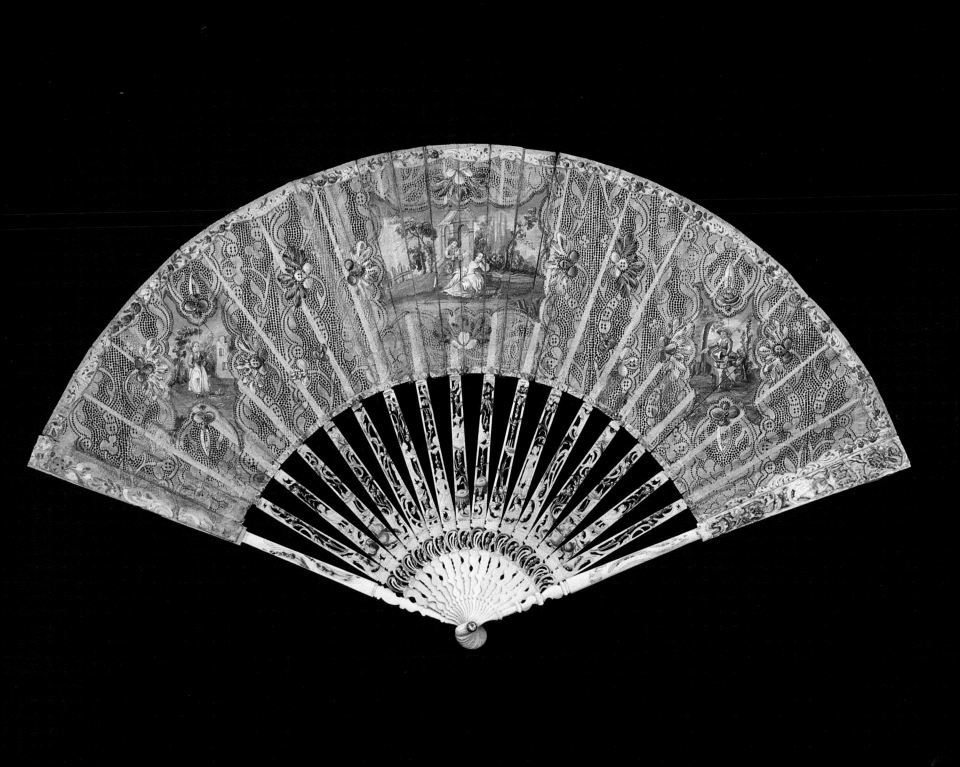

VI Grand Tour

The tour recommended for aristocratic young Englishmen took them from Calais through France, Germany, and Switzerland, then south to Italy and Rome. In Rome, galleries offered paintings and engravings of the famous monuments and city views,[1] many of which were reproduced on fans. Fan-makers used a variety of materials for the sticks – ivory and bone, lacquer and horn – but the leaf was invariably made from skin. The fans cover a period from the mid-eighteenth century to the first quarter of the nineteenth.[2]

1. As shown in *Picture Gallery with Views of Modern Rome, 1757* by Giovanni Paolo Pannini (1691-1765) in the Museum of Fine Arts, Boston (1975.805).

2. Other grand tour fans in the collection are *Trevi Fountain* (1976.345, Appendix) and *Quirinali Palace* (1976.349, Appendix).

Ivory guard stick
Italy, 1780s
1976.349, (Appendix)

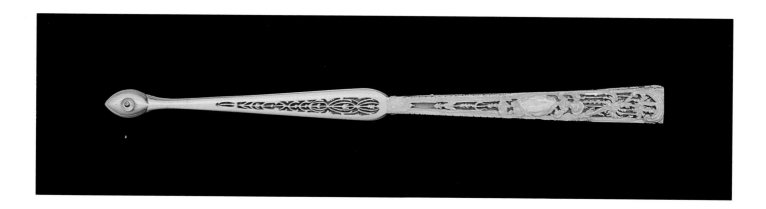

St. Peter's Basilica *(cat. 61)*

Italy, 1750-80
Skin leaf (double), painted in gouache and touches of India ink
15 red lacquer sticks with delicate gilt chinoiserie detail
Large bone thumbguards, mother-of-pearl washers at rivet
Guard: 29 cm. Maximum open: 52.5 cm.   Arc. 140 °
Acc. no. 1976.346

This view of Saint Peter's Basilica with forecourt and Bernini colonnades shows more than the contemporary visitor could have seen, for many medieval buildings still stood that would have obscured such a vista. The fan painter probably adapted one of the engravings by Giovanni Battista Piranesi (1720-1778), whose views of Rome generated many souvenirs of the Grand Tour. The viewpoint is a little lower and closer than Piranesi's and slightly off-center.[1] Castel Sant'Angelo is depicted on the reverse. The red border shows the leaf was extended at top and sides for new sticks.

Rome exerted a magnetic draw on young gentlemen completing their educations and on collectors scouting for antiquities. The Apollo Belvedere and the Laocoön at the Vatican were only the most famous of the treasures to be seen. The souvenir from Rome, like the medieval pilgrim's shell from Santiago da Compostela in Spain, proved the journey had been made and implied the acquisition of culture.

1. See Arthur M. Hind, *Giovanni Battista Piranesi* (London: 1922), plate LXIV (St. Peter's, with Forecourt and Colonnades), p. 120, pl. I (birds-eye view).

Classical Ruins (cat. 62)

England(?), 1740s
Skin leaf (single), etched and painted in watercolor
19 narrow ivory sticks, pierced and gilded; guard pierced and carved
Guard: 28 cm. Maximum open: 44 cm. Arc. 115° Acc. no. 01.6689
Bequest of Mrs. Arthur Croft

A few grandiose ruins of the classical past, overgrown with vegetation and crumbling away, are arranged like a stage set and peopled by very strange actors. Some appear to be peasants, others wear long, togalike garments. A woman in the center has been given a conical hat in the chinoiserie style. The scene offers an interesting contrast to those based on Piranesi engravings. While the latter served to remind the tourist of what he had seen, the fanciful ruins shown here are more likely to have inspired such a journey.

The leaf is mounted *à l'anglaise*. A few touches of gilt decorate the leaf and the sticks.

Provenance: Gardner Brewer

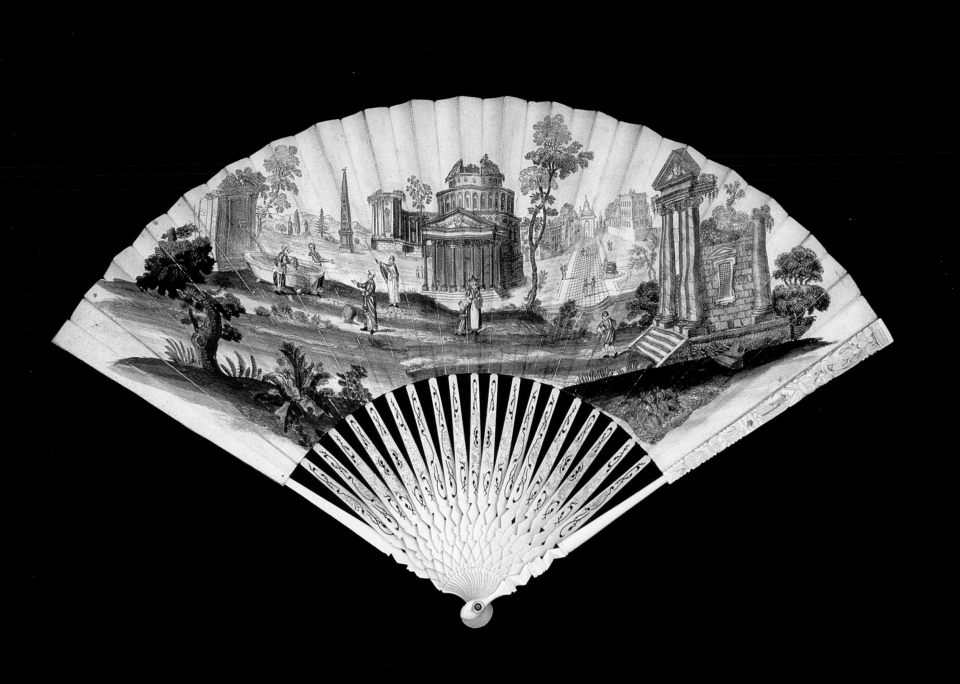

The Temple of Minerva Medica *(cat. 63)*

Italy, 1775-80
Skin leaf (double), painted in gouache
12 horn sticks with gilt-silver decoration; guards with incised decoration
Guard: 27 cm. Maximum open: 52.5 cm. Arc: 150° Acc. no. 1976.348

The crumbling monuments depicted on the leaf are but three of the hundreds that stirred the imagination of Europeans in the mid-eighteenth century and drew them to the seat of Roman culture.

It is probable that the fan painter used Piranesi engravings as the basis for these souvenir fans.[1] A noticeable difference, however, is the absence of the antlike human figures that give the Piranesi engravings such a dramatic sense of scale.[2] The Arch of Titus is shown at left, the Temple of Saturn at right, with the Arch of Septimus Severus in the background. The mysterious ruin in the center is known as the Temple of Minerva Medica. The Roman goddess was worshipped for her healing powers, and temple excavations have revealed what have been interpreted as ex-voto objects. The fan painter has exercised artistic license by depicting these sites in a more picturesque manner than they would have appeared at the time. Their massive, crumbling, and overgrown character has been romantically exaggerated.

The disciplined organization of the leaf, with its delicate Adamesque ornament derived from Roman grotesque, shows that the decoration no less than the images was indebted to the classical past.

1. See Arthur M. Hind, *Giovanni Battista Piranesi* (London, 1922), plate LIII, 98,II (The Arch of Titus); plate LIX, 110,I (The Temple of Saturn).

2. *Ibid.*, plate XLI, 74,I (The Temple of Minerva Medica).

162

Vesuvius (cat. 64)

Italy, c. 1820
Skin leaf (double), painted in gouache
20 bone sticks, pierced and carved; carved ivory guards
Diamond paste stud at rivet
Guard: 29 cm. Maximum open: 56 cm. Arc: 170° Acc. no. 1976.350

The background of this souvenir fan is deep green, setting off the orange of Vesuvius erupting in the central cartouche. In style and composition this scene is closely related to similar paintings by Joseph Wright of Derby (1734-1797). At left, peasant musicians serenade a statue of the Virgin, while a boy looks on. At the right, two women groom the hair of a third woman and a little girl.

A quiescent volcano is pictured on the reverse, gently smoking above a sunny Bay of Naples. In the left-hand vignette, a peasant family prepares and eats pasta, while at right a couple dances to castanets and the music of two seated musicians.

The Roman painter Bartolommeo Pinelli (1781-1835) popularized the subject of local peasant costume in his *Raccolta di Costumi pittoreschi*, a book of engravings. His work was carried on by Pietro Fabris, a Venetian active in Naples.

The germ of the classical revival lay in the excavations at Herculaneum and Pompeii. It was considered essential for young gentlemen making the Grand Tour to visit Naples. The sinister connection between Vesuvius and the buried cities was reinforced by volcanic eruptions in 1766-67, 1779, 1794, and 1822.

Exhibitions

Fans from the Oldham Collection, Museum of Fine Arts, Boston, November 25, 1977 - March 5, 1978.

Publications

Esther Oldham, "Fans East and West," *Antiques* (February 1948): 127, ill.

VII Memory Aids

English publishers, especially, found a receptive market for leaves printed with detailed information that could be carried for reference as needed. Surviving fans are printed with the words of songs, stagecoach routes, parlor games, saints' calendars, botanical information, even the names of box holders at the opera. An appropriate fan was available to reinforce the memory in almost any situation.

Guard stick, bone and wood, (cat. 68)
Germany, c. 1795
1976.332

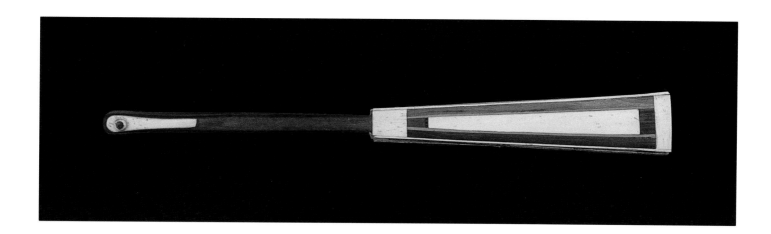

Cockade Calendar *(cat. 65)*

France, 1774
White silk leaf (single), letter-press printed and painted in watercolor
Round wood handle, retracting into wooden case banded with ivory
Handle: 14.5 cm. Diameter: 23 cm. Acc. no. 43.2097
Elizabeth Day McCormick Collection

The fan's pleated silk leaf, when extended from its case by means of a brass lever and a cord, opens to 360 degrees, forming a perfect cockade. It is printed with the names of saints and major church celebrations for each day of the year 1774. Butterflies are painted between the months, and a floral swag border and dentated edging complete the decoration.

The fan's circular shape, represented by several examples in the collection,[1] perpetuates the ancient flabellum form. Its adaptation as a calendar and a memory aid is unusual.[2]

1. Other cockades are listed in the Appendix: 1976.388, 47.1528, and, as a *parasolette*, 1976.254.

2. *Flabellum* derives from the Latin *flare* ("to blow"). A feather flabellum is carried before the pope on state occasions.

Malbrouk *(cat. 66)*

France, c. 1782
Paper leaf (double), découpé, etched, and painted in watercolor
14 bone sticks with minimal painting; guard backed with red foil
Guard: 26.5 cm. Maximum open: 48 cm. Arc: 145° Acc. no. 1976.231

This is not a serious commemorative fan honoring a dead military hero but rather an *aide-mémoire*, with the words of a popular song on the reverse. John Churchill, the first Duke of Marlborough, or Malbrouk, as he was called in France, lived from 1650 to 1722. He had been dead for more than fifty years when this fan was made. In the interim he had become legendary and the subject of a well-known ballad. Marie Antoinette is said to have sung it to her children, and perhaps for this reason it became a popular favorite.

The leaf has been stamped with a filet lace design. Malbrouk's body lies on a catafalque, draped with flags and decorated with cannon and armor. Mourning women and a child encircle his bier. In the right cartouche, Malbrouk takes leave of his wife as his page holds his helmet. At left, his wife, draped in mourning, stands with his page and his horse. Malbrouk's wife is modishly dressed in the style of the early 1780s. Malbrouk, on the other hand, both alive and dead, wears a wig in the style of circa 1700. The fan has an edge like a lace doily.

The nineteen verses of the song *"La Mort de Mr d'Malbrouk"* are written out on the reverse.[1] About ten bars of the tune are inscribed, with many verses. The story in capsule:

Malbrouk s'en vat en guerre	Malbrouk goes to war
Mironton ton ton [refrain]	Mironton ton ton
Ne sait pas quand reviendra . . .	Doesn't know when he will return . . .
Madame à sa tour monte	Madame ascends her tower
Elle voit venir son Page	Sees his page coming
De noir tout habillé . . .	All dressed in black . . .
Aux nouvelles que j'apporte	At the news I bring
Vox beaux yeux vont pleurer	Your beautiful eyes will weep . . .
Mironton ton ton . . .[2]	Mironton ton ton . . .

1. A similar fan appears in Lady Charlotte Schreiber, *Fans and Fan Leaves* (London, 1888, 1890), English nos. 53-54, Foreign nos. 16-17; and in Lionel Cust, *Catalogue of the Collection of Fans . . . of the British Museum* (London, 1893), no. 200.

2. The song has been traced to a medieval ballad, popular before 1200. Its application to Marlborough, the commander-in-chief of the English and Dutch armies, was made at the time of the disastrous battle of Malplaquet in 1709, when the allies defeated the French troops during the War of the Spanish Succession (1702-12). See Edith Gaines, "A la Malbrough," *Antiques* (August 1962), 172.

Exhibitions

Fans from the Oldham Collection, Museum of Fine Arts, Boston, November 25, 1977 - March 5, 1978.

Publications

Esther Oldham, "Sheer Beauty: Early Rare Fans," *Antiques* (August 1962): 164, ill.

Botanical Orders (cat. 67)

England, 1792
Paper leaf (double), etched, engraved and painted in watercolor
18 plain ivory sticks
Mother-of-pearl buttons at rivet
Guard: 25 cm. Maximum open: 46 cm. Arc: 155° Acc. no. 1976.178

Two of the usual methods of classifying plants are by their leaf shape and arrangement and by their flower structure. This charming late-eighteenth-century English botanical fan illustrates both methods. Twenty-four variations of plant reproductive structures are illustrated on the obverse and listed on the reverse with the Latin designation and English translation of each category, along with an example of the type. For example, number three is a triandria, or triple stamen, typical of the iris. The top and bottom bands show various leaf shapes, labelled with descriptions such as "sharp," "blunt," and "scalloped." The sides of the fan illustrate the arrangement of leaves on the stem. In the center are three flowers with their sections carefully labelled. The principal parts of the flower are enumerated in a list, enclosed within a calligraphic frame, located in the central portion of the reverse. Below is the second stanza from the fourth canto of Charles Darwin's *Botanic Garden* (V.I.). The publisher's imprint reads: "Published as the Act directs, July 21, 1792, by Sarah Ashton, No. 28 Little Britain, London." [1]

The fan's fresh color and delicate forms are secondary to its educational message. Where rococo flowers on other fans serve a decorative purpose, those on botanical fans are regimented and labeled for classification. The viewer is invited to look closely, to study, to count leaves and compare shapes. The goal is an extension of knowledge through classification and observation.

The same scientific purpose lay behind the Royal Botanic Gardens of Kew, near London. Where parks had been designed for aesthetic enjoyment and recreation, these new gardens, established in 1759, promoted the science of botany. Sir Joseph Banks (1743-1820) served as, honorary director, encouraging research and an international exchange of information. In Paris, the Jardin du Roi also promoted the natural sciences, under the direction of Georges LeClerc, Comte de Buffon. Both men and both institutions were exponents of the Enlightenment. The botanical fan attests to the wide dissemination of the new ideas: they had penetrated at least as far as the drawing room. [2]

1. The Museum of Fine Arts collection includes another example of the same leaf, unmounted, with a slight variation in the imprint (1976.549).

2. *Botanical Orders* appears as nos. 69 and 70 in the English volume of Lady Charlotte Schreiber's *Fans and Fan Leaves* (London, 1888), and in Lionel Cust, *Catalogue of the Collection of Fans of the British Museum* (London, 1893), p. 96.

Provenance: DeWitt Clinton Cohen

Exhibitions

Fans from the Oldham Collection, Museum of Fine Arts, Boston, November 25, 1977 - March 5, 1978.

Publications

Esther Oldham, "Unmounted Fan Leaves," in *Spinning Wheel* (September 1964): 20, ill.

German Song *(cat. 68)*

Germany, c. 1795
Paper leaf (double), etched and painted in watercolor, with applied brass sequins
11 wood sticks (pallisander?); guard with inlaid bone and light wood on guard head
Bone thumbguard
Guard: 27.5 cm. Maximum open: 50.5 cm. Arc: 150°
Acc. no. 1976.332

A central scene of seven figures in a landscape and exterior scenes of dancing men are separated by sequin-bordered medallions containing a German song about the fickleness of love:

Doch vierzehn Tag später da ist es vorbei
da singen und pfeiffen sie schon eins und zwei; eins und zwei;
doch ohne ohne Treu.

But two weeks later all is over,
They will sing and whistle their own tune:
one and two, one and two.
There is no faithfulness.

Sie wünschen den Liebling, sie wünschen den Tanz,
wünchen die Hochzeit, sie wünchen den Kranz: eins und zwei, eins und zwei, ohne Treu.

They wish for a lover, they wish for the dance,
They wish for the wedding, they wish for the wedding wreath:
one and two, one and two,
There is no faithfulness.

Der Tanz ist sehr lustig,
er hebet die Füss
und ist mir zum Tanzen der Liebste
gewiss, der Liebste gewiss.

The dance is lots of fun,
It makes you lift your feet
And I'm sure of my lover when
he dances with me.

The costumes of the five women are of special interest, showing the 1790s style. Typical of the time is the gown of thin fabric, with a high waistline beneath the bust. Over their flowing hair, the women wear feathered turbans. They bear a striking resemblance to the figures of Nicolaus von Heideloff (1761-1837) in the periodical *Gallery of Fashion*.

Exhibitions

Fans from the Oldham Collection, Museum of Fine Arts, Boston, November 25, 1977 - March 5, 1978.

Fanology *(cat. 69)*

England, 1797. Published by Robert Clarke, No. 26, Strand, London
Paper leaf (double), stipple engraved
18 wood sticks; polished guards
Guard: 26 cm. Maximum open: 46.5 cm. Arc: (unmeasurable)
Acc. no. 1976.311

This fan, which facilitated a parlor game, was published by Robert Clarke, "Fan Maker," who must have hoped that a system of silent communication with fans would promote sales. The title and overt purpose are stated in the center: "Fanology or the Ladies Conversation Fan. This fan Improves the Friendship & sets forth a Plan For Ladies to Chit Chat & hold the tongue."

The game, invented by Charles Francis Badini, depended on equating five numbers with five fan postions: (1) the fan to the right arm; (2) the fan to the left arm; (3) the fan to the bosom; (4) the fan to the lips; (5) the fan to the head. By dividing the alphabet into five letter groups (omitting the letter J), each letter of the alphabet could be indicated by moving the fan in two positions. The first position would signal the number of the alphabetical group, the second the place of the letter within its group. For example, the letter D belongs to the first group (fan to the right arm), and is the fourth letter in its group (fan to the lips). Names could be spelled out in that way, or short words – but not at lightning speed.

The same system could be applied to "Familiar questions and their respective answers," presented on the fan's reverse.

Another fanology fan was published by William Cock of 42, Pall Mall, six months after Clarke's fan, attesting to the popularity of this genre. It was entitled *The Telegraph of Cupid in this Fan.* As the title suggests, it was more directly coquettish, and, as a result, the questions and the answers are more arch. The fan is described and illustrated in Lady Charlotte Schreiber's *Fans and Fan Leaves* (London, 1888) as English 147-48. It has lovely paired sticks of ivory and sandalwood and is delicately colored. It was acquired by Lady Schreiber's great grandson, Lord Oranmore and Browne.[2]

1. The celebrated nineteenth-century Parisian fan-maker, J. Duvelleroy, copyrighted English instructions for another, more rapid way of communicating with fans. It was based on, but differed from, a Spanish system developed by Fenella and published in German by a Frau Bartholomäus (see George Woolliscroft Rhead: *History of the Fan* [Philadelphia, 1910], pp. 136-37). While this "silent flirtation" no doubt advanced many an affair of the heart, it may have caused its share of misunderstandings. Both players had to know the rules, and the manipulation had to be precise. A fan placed behind the head meant "Don't forget me"; placed on the left ear it signaled "I wish to get rid of you." See Bertha de Vere Green, *A Collector's Guide to Fans* (London, 1975), p. 156.
2. See Nancy Armstrong, *The Book of Fans* (Surrey, 1978), p. 13, ill.

Exhibitions
Fans from the Oldham Collection, Museum of Fine Arts, Boston, November 25, 1977 - March 5, 1978.

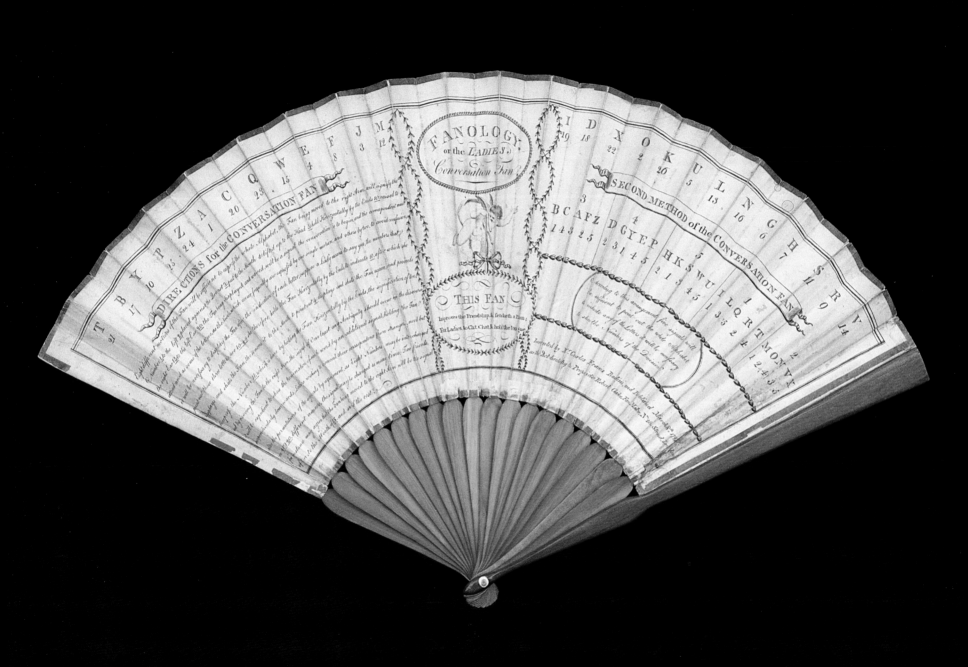

FANOLOGY
or the LADIES
Conversation Fan

THIS FAN
Improves the Friendship & setteth a Fan;
For Ladies, to Chit Chat & hold the tongue

DIRECTIONS for the CONVERSATION FAN

SECOND METHOD of the CONVERSATION FAN

T B Y P Z A C Q W E F J M
3 17 10 25 24 I 20 23 15 4 8 3 12

I D X O K U L N G H S R V
19 18 22 2 26 5 13 16 6 7 11 9 14

B C A F Z   D G Y E P   H K S W U I   L Q R T M O N V
1 4 3 2 5   2 3 1 4 5   2 1 3 4 5   1 3 5 2 4   1 2 4 3 3

Liberty Song *(cat. 70)*

France, 1789-92
Paper leaf (double), etched, engraved (inscription), and painted in watercolor
14 bone sticks
Bone washer at rivet
Guard: 27 cm. Maximum open: 50.5 cm. Arc: 160° Acc. no. 1976.234

Intended as an *aide-mémoire*, the *dominotier*-style leaf is printed with the words of a French Revolutionary song to be sung to a popular tune of the day, *"Adieu donc Dame Françoise."* The accompanying image shows a statue of Liberty in the center. In her right hand she holds a Freemason's plummet and triangle. In her left hand is a staff, surmounted by a Phrygian (Liberty) cap, and a tablet inscribed, *"Droit de L'Homme."* Liberty stands on a pedestal, which is also inscribed: *"Liberté, égalité, fraternité, unité."* Dancing figures surround the statue with garlands and baskets of flowers. The six song verses express revolutionary, anti-aristocratic sentiment and contrast natural nobility with an inherited nobility that goes no deeper than the paper that documents it.[1]

(Stanza 3)

Un comte avoit sa Noblesse	A count had his Nobility
Bien roulée en parchemin.	Rolled up in parchment.
Un maudit Rat pièce à pièce	A cursed Rat, piece by piece
A rongé tout le vélin.	Gnawed all the vellum.
Pourquoi diable sa Noblesse	Why the devil is his Nobility
Est-elle de parchemin?	Made of parchment?

(Stanza 4)

Nos droits sont dans la nature	Our rights are from Nature
La raison les recouvra . . .	Reason will recover them . . .

(Stanza 5)

Je connois une patrone	I know a patron
Qui se nomme Liberté	Whose name is Liberty.
A ses Elus elle donne	To her elect she gives
Force, gloire et sûreté . . .	Strength, glory and security . . .

(Stanza 6)

. . . J'ai juré de mourir libre	. . . I have sworn to die free
Et je tiendrai mon serment.	And I will keep my word.

1. The same leaf appears as Foreign no. 69 in Lady Charlotte Schreiber's *Fans and Fan Leaves* (London, 1890). Lady Schreiber's example is identical, except that the tablet held by Liberty is blank. It also appears in Lionel Cust, *Catalogue of the Collection of Fans . . . of the British Museum* (London, 1893), no. 100.

Publications

Esther Oldham, "Fans of the Paper Stainers: Dominotier and Imagier," *Hobbies* (December 1959): 28-29, ill.

LaFayette's Promise of Liberty (cat. 71)

France, c. 1790
Shiny paper leaf (double), etched, engraved (inscription), and painted in watercolor
13 bone sticks; carved guard
Guard: 27 cm. Maximum open: 48 cm. Arc: 140-45°
Acc. no. 1976.235

Marie Joseph Paul Yves Roch Gilbert du Motier, Marquis de LaFayette, was born in 1757. His wealth and great family connections helped him to obtain a commission as a major-general in the Continental Army during the American Revolution and rapidly advanced his political career in France. He never misused his power, however, and his role in the French Revolution seems to have been a genuinely idealistic one. Elected to the Estates-General in 1789, he drafted a Declaration of Rights, modeled after Thomas Jefferson's Declaration of Independence. He was chosen colonel-general of the National Guard and proposed the tricolor for the flag, which remains the symbol of France today. During the period 1789-92, he tried to oppose revolutionary excesses and was branded a traitor by the radical Jacobins. Impeached and proscribed, he fled, was captured by Austrian troops, and spent five years in prisons in Prussia and Austria. He was freed in 1797 and returned to France, where he continued to work for his ideals of Liberty until his death in 1834. Few public figures have commanded such respect at home and abroad.

On the fan leaf, LaFayette in the uniform of an officer stands by the flaming altar marked by the fleur-de-lis of France. A crowned, robed figure opposite him holds a branch. Manifestly not Louis XVI,[1] the personnage is female, wearing a gown and classical sandals. She personifies France or Liberty, as the words of the song indicate:

Pour la rendre heureuse à jamais	To make her happy forever
Un héro promet à la France	A hero promises France
Que rien ne pourra desormais	That nothing can henceforth
Détruire son indépendance . . .	Destroy her independence . . .

The presence of a couple on either side of the central pair is explained by subsequent stanzas of the song. Not only political but personal liberty is promised, including the freedom to marry for love. Anteros, brother of Eros, hovers above the altar holding a torch, his attribute, which symbolizes requited or shared love. Turning away from the *tristes noeuds* ("sad knots") of arranged marriages,

On verra les coeurs amoureux	One will see loving hearts
S'én chaînant au gré de leurs feux	Linking up according to their ardor,
Donner librement leur parole.	To give their word freely.

1. An example with twisted sticks appears in Lady Charlotte Schreiber, *Fans and Fan Leaves* (London, 1890), Foreign no. 53. The crowned figure was identified as Louis XVI.

Exhibitions

Fans from the Oldham Collection, Museum of Fine Arts, Boston, November 25, 1977 - March 5, 1978.

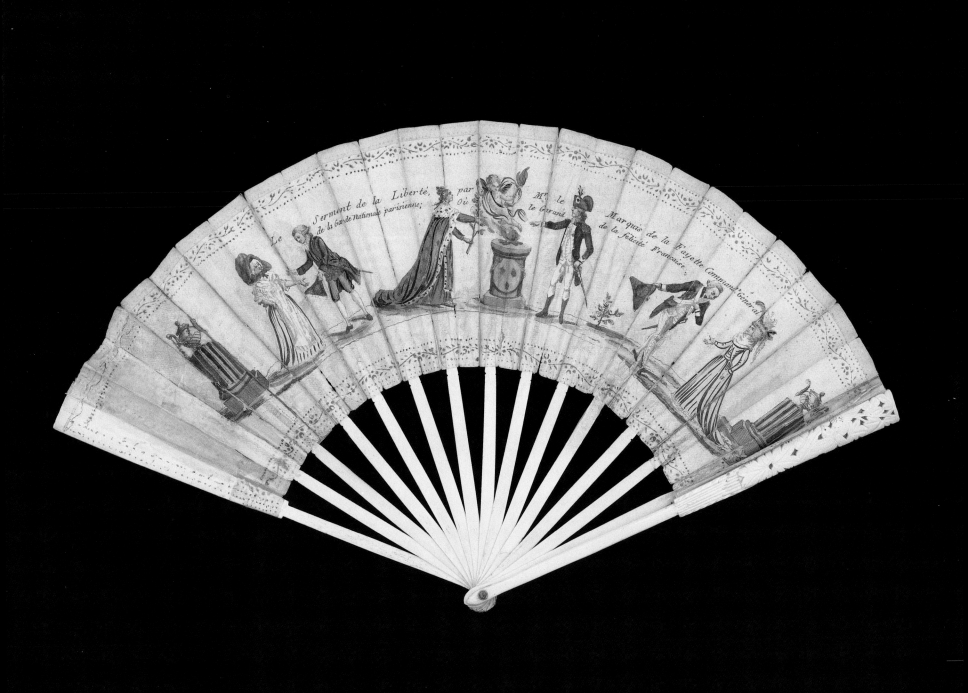

Le Serment de la Liberté, par Mr. le Marquis de la Fayette Commandant Général de la Garde Nationale parisienne; Où le Garand de la félicité Française

The Oracle (cat. 72)

England, c. 1800
Paper leaf (double), engraved and painted in watercolor
18 wood sticks
Mother-of-pearl washer at rivet
Guard: 25 cm. Maximum open: 45 cm. Arc: 145° Acc. no. 1976.313

This fortune-telling fan is a kind of parlor game played with a pin. The numerous perforations of the leaf show it was a popular diversion. The title, "Oracle," hangs between two winged figures and a Book of Fate. A wheel with numbers is at center, pierced with many pinholes. The "Explication" is at left, and "Example" at right. Numbered questions are at either side.

The system works by two numbers: the first is the number of the question selected; the second is determined by laying a pin on the wheel of fortune. This number leads the questioner to a list of deities. The questioner then uses the first number to select a deity within that list.

Turning to the reverse, which has columns headed by the name and face of a deity, the questioner again applies the number selected by the pin on the wheel of fortune. This gives the answer to the question put to the Oracle.

The Oracle appeared in Lady Charlotte Schreiber's *Fans and Fan Leaves* (London, 1888), as English no. 150-51. The English version, possibly published by John Cock, J. P. Crowder and Co., was followed later by a French version, of which numerous examples survive.[2]

1. This fan also appeared in Lionel Cust, *Catalogue of the Collection of Fans . . . of the British Museum* (London, 1893), no. 64.

2. The collection includes another fan with a question-and-answer game, written in Roman dialect (1976.351, Appendix).

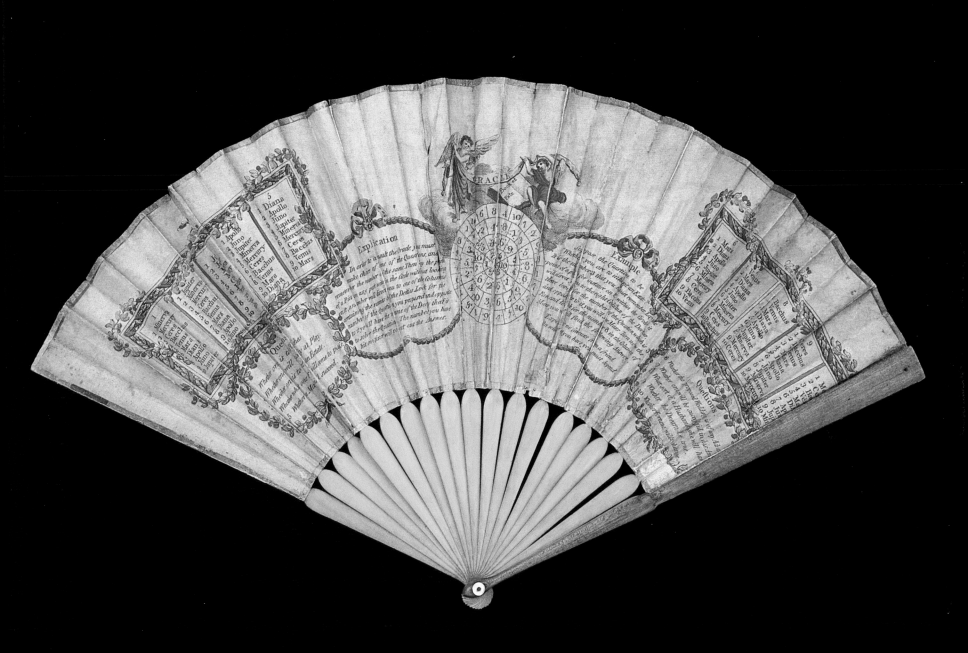

VIII Romantic Revivals

To escape the encroaching effects of industrialization, many nineteenth-century artists chose subjects removed in time or place from their own. Depending on artistic temperament and purpose, their interpretations were heroic, sentimental, or simply trivial. Earlier fan forms, like the brisé, reappeared. Quaintness was cultivated.

Painting styles were as various as subject matter, from the heavily painted *Moorish Wedding* to the porcelain perfection of *Blindman's Buff*.

Ivory guard stick, (cat. 77)
France, c. 1875
1976.271

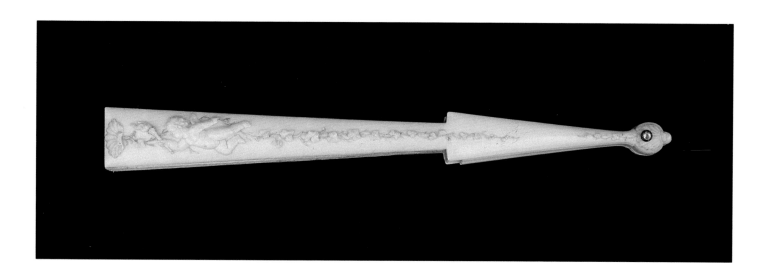

Melrose Abbey *(cat. 73)*

England, c. 1825
Brisé-type, 22 horn blades, painted in watercolor and gilded
Brown silk connecting ribbon
Blue "jeweled" studs at rivet
Guard: 17.5 cm. Maximum open: 33 cm. Arc: 170° Acc. no. 1976.317

Romantic interest in ruins, particularly churches, was intense in the early nineteenth century. The painting of a ruined Gothic cloister is complemented by the blades, which end in gilded crocket shapes.[1] Gilt dots resembling piqué work decorate the crockets and form a line under the connecting ribbon. The guards end in a trefoil shape at the rivet.

Melrose Abbey on the Tweed River in Scotland combined picturesque ruins with historical associations. Built on the site of a seventh-century Columban monastery, it was destroyed and rebuilt at least three times. The heart of Robert I, "The Bruce," king of Scotland from 1306 to 1329, was buried at the high altar. Its handsome sixteenth-century ruins exerted a powerful attraction at the time of the Gothic revival. While there is some question that it is Melrose Abbey depicted here, the image is representative of many such ruins that served as tourist meccas in the 1820s.

1. The collection includes another fan exploiting the crocket shape (43.2095, Appendix). Alternating blade terminals in an attenuated crocket form enclose classical and contemporary figures.

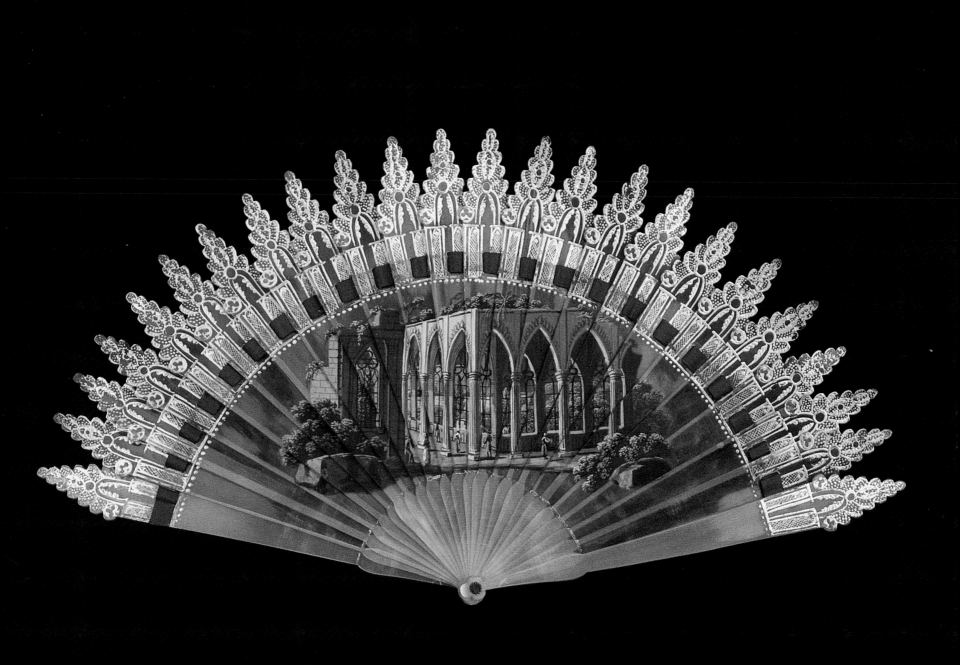

The Engagement (cat. 74)

Europe, c. 1830
Skin leaf (double), etched, painted in gouache
23 ivory sticks, pierced and carved, gilded, backed with iridescent mother-of-pearl
Diamond paste studs at rivet
Guard: 32.5 cm. Maximum open: 59 cm. Arc: 165° Acc. no. 1976.342

Printed lace winds and twists on a striped blue background around a central scene depicting three figures on a terrace. A gray-haired man, possibly a clergyman or a lawyer, shows a young man's portrait to a young woman and a bald-headed man. A distant townscape, Italianate in character, is visible beyond a balustrade. A trompe l'oeil fly rests on a section of lace. On the reverse, another tangled mass of printed lace surrounds a painted "picture" of a loving couple in a landscape. The picture has a flowered blue background.

An instructive comparison can be made between this fan and another in the collection (cat. no. 10), in which the lace is painted, not printed, and which undoubtedly dates from the eighteenth century. The example here was called a "gentleman's fan," perhaps because of its size. Fans of these dimensions were used as sun shades. The presence of the printed lace and certain inconsistencies in the costumes speak for a nineteenth-century date. If this is correct, this fan is an interesting example of the fans made after 1830 that imitated the fans of a century earlier, possibly with the intention of deceiving.

Publications

Estger Oldham, "Sheer Beauty: Early Lace Fans," *Antiques* (August 1962): 163, ill.

Oldham, "The Fan: A Gentleman's Accessory," *The Connoisseur* (March 1950): 16, ill.

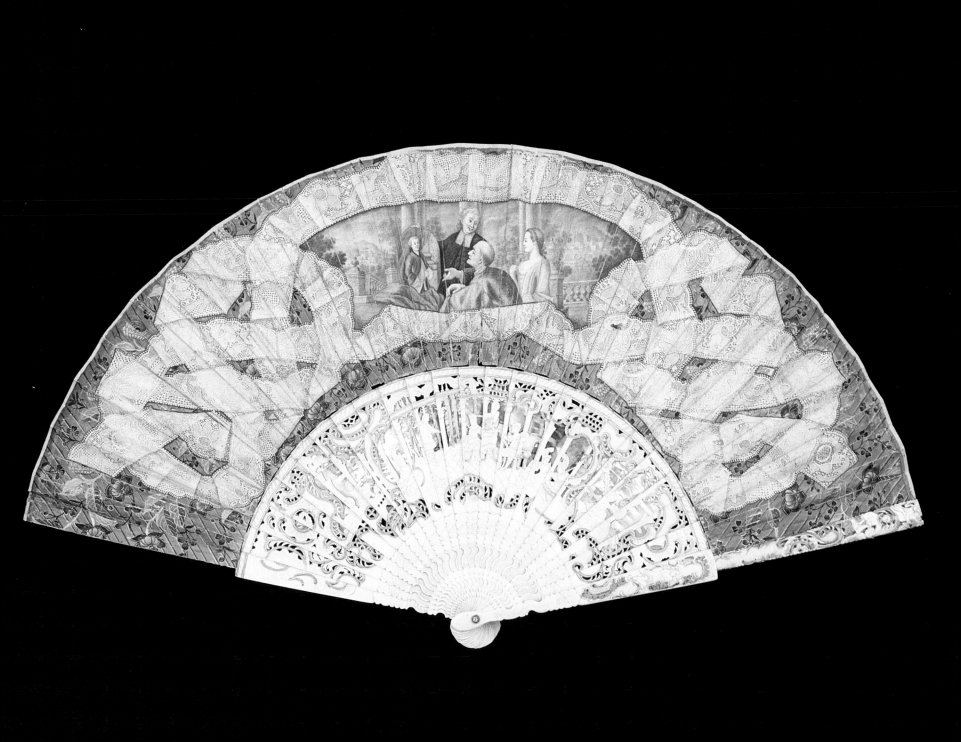

The Embarkation for Cythera (cat. 75)

France, for Spanish market, mid-19th century
Paper leaf (double), painted in watercolor, lithographed, gilded and
embossed after Antoine Watteau (1684-1721)
12 heavy mother-of-pearl sticks, pierced and incised with cornucopia
motifs and ogival arches in applied gilt
Brass button at rivet and ornate ring
Guard: 28 cm. Maximum open: 52 cm. Arc: 160° Acc. no. 56.131
Gift of Miss Mary Lee in memory of Miss Alice Lee

Antoine Watteau's painting of 1717, *L'Embarquement pour Cythère*, now at the Louvre, inspired this lithographed fan leaf. The resemblances and differences are equally instructive. Missing in the fan is the painting's quality of enchantment. The mist has been dissolved to reveal all in sharp focus. The figures are squatter, heavier; the colors are brighter, with much more gold. The horizon has been lowered, the foreground shortened. Many more figures, especially *amorini*, have been added (partially to fill out the width of the leaf for the fan's horizontal format). Embossed gilt frames enclose two lateral cartouches of peasants in romantic poses, while small reserves at the upper edge show animals, again framed in gold with gilt fringes.

The shiny gray paper of the reverse is printed with three gold frames enclosing a boating party (*center*), a romantic couple (*left*), and two women examining a letter (*right*). The nineteenth-century interest in period costumes is evident in the three eras represented here: Renaissance (*left*), seventeenth century (*center*), and eighteenth century (*right*).

A fan in the collection showing the interest in Spanish costume is illustrated in the Appendix (43.1293).

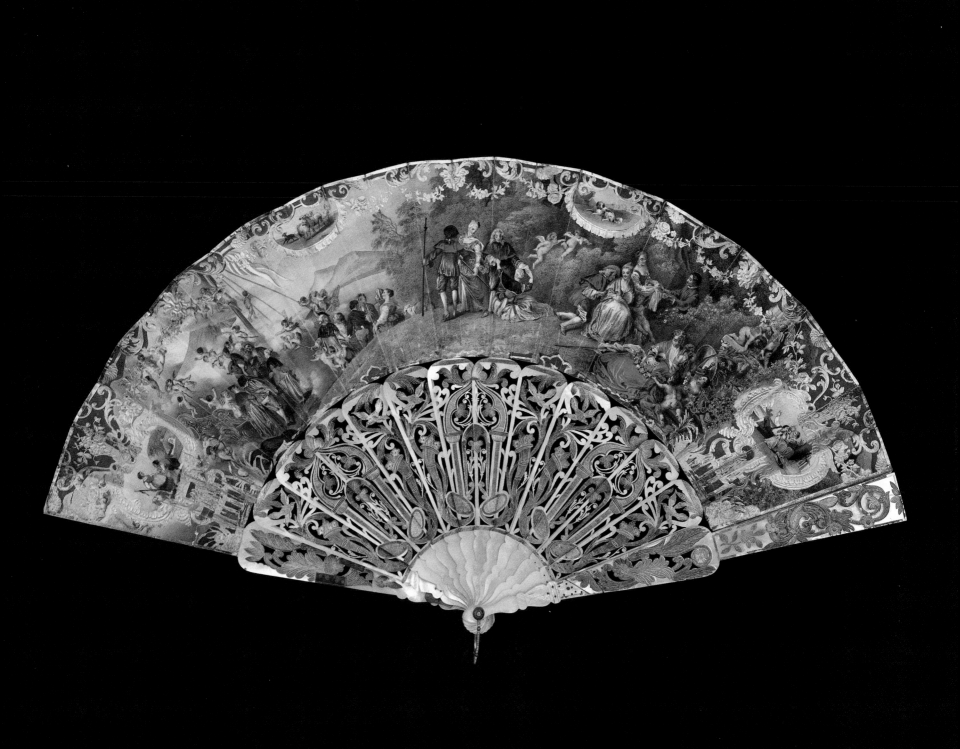

Fancy Dress *(cat. 76)*

England, for Spanish market(?), c. 1860
Paper leaf (double), lithographed, painted in gouache, and gilded
12 wide japanned sticks of papier-mâché, painted in oil and gilded
with mother-of-pearl inlay
Gilt ring with dependent red silk tassel
Guard: 29 cm. Maximum open: 51 cm. Arc: 165° Acc. no. 1976.283

Couples in neo-rococo costumes dance, go boating, play with a dog, and admire flowers on this mid-nineteenth-century fan. The banality of the leaf contrasts sharply with the remarkable sticks that support it, showing another costume party on the central sticks. Five figures, again in eighteenth-century costume, are portrayed against a black japanned surface. Their faces are slightly three-dimensional. Their costumes are made of thin sheets of mother-of-pearl with surface details added. The musical party takes place under Moorish arches with fine gilt tracery embellished by bits of mother-of-pearl. Three of the guard surfaces also show heavily gilded figures with three-dimensional faces, reminiscent of the "Mandarin" fans with faces of painted applied ivory. The material of the sticks and their decoration is evidence of the technological developments in England that resulted in a flourishing japanning industry between 1825 and 1860.

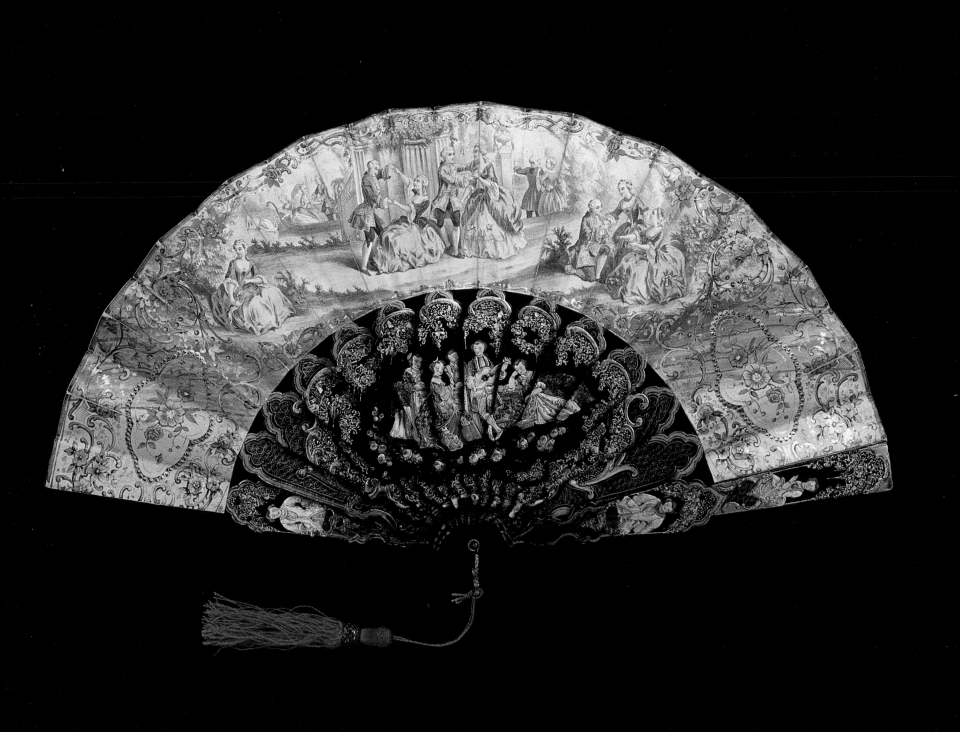

Moorish Wedding (cat. 77)

France, Paris (Duvelleroy), c. 1875
Skin leaf (double), painted in oils, signed (right) "Victor Eeckhout, Tanger"
13 ivory sticks, carved in high relief, gilt details
Diamond paste studs at rivet
Guard: 28 cm. Maximum open: 54 cm. Arc: 170° Acc. no. 1976.271

A Moorish wedding procession advances across the leaf from right to left. The heavily veiled bride, the towering dowry, and the retinue beating drums were details to stir nineteenth-century imaginations. Interest in distant lands and customs was stimulated early in the century by Napoleon's Egyptian campaign and by the development of railways, which made it easier to travel to distant lands.

The overlapping ivory sticks are carved with a scene of the Toilette of Venus. *Putti* hold a mirror, jewels, and garlands. The image of Anteros with a flaming torch on one of the guards indicates that the fan was intended for a wedding. The coronet and monogram of the viscountess for whom the fan was made are painted in gouache on the reverse. The fan came in a maroon leather box, stamped in gold with "J. Duvelleroy, Paris. By Appointment London: 167, Regent Street, 167."

1. The artist, Victor Eeckhout, was born in Antwerp in 1821, and died in 1879. He exhibited in Paris and Brussels.

Publications

Esther Oldham, "Wedding and Betrothal Fans," in Fan Guild of Boston, *Fan Leaves* (Boston, 1961), VII, pp. 6-7, ill.

Oldham, "Wedding and Betrothal Fans – Love and Marriage Go Together," *The Antiques Journal* (July 1959): 34, ill.

Pastoral Reprise (cat. 78)

France, Paris (Duvelleroy), 1880s
Silk leaf (double), painted in gouache, signed "Loch", decorated with brass, steel, and multicolored sequins
14 ivory sticks, machine pierced and decorated with gilt-silver and silver piqué work
Mother-of-pearl button at rivet
Guard: 28 cm. Maximum open: 53 cm. Arc: 145° Acc. no. 1976.269

This beautiful late-Victorian reprise reflects the eighteenth-century manner. A couple in pastoral costume are depicted in a misty landscape. The delicate pastel tones of the painting complement the pink surround and the musical trophy at right. Very small multicolored sequins are used for restrained sparkle within the scene and as a decorative border. The swan with outspread wings provides an art nouveau accent.

The artist may have been Miss Alice Helen Loch, an accomplished British landscape watercolorist and winner in an 1878 competition in London.[1]

1. See Nancy Armstrong, *A Collector's History of Fans* (London, 1974), p. 196.

Blindman's Buff *(cat. 79)*

France, Paris (Duvelleroy?), 1890s
Skin leaf (single), silk lined; painted in watercolor and signed "G. Neitey"
15 mother-of-pearl (abalone) sticks, pierced and gilded
Gilt ring at rivet
Guard: 29.5 cm. Maximum open: 51 cm. Arc: 140° Acc. no. 1976.270

Card players in the right background pause in their game to watch five adults engaged in a coy and prettified version of the old *colin-maillard,* or blindman's buff. The players wear neo-rococo costumes in an "eighteenth-century" salon with period furniture. The subject matter and mood of this elegant fan would have made it the perfect accessory to carry at one of the costume balls popular in the nineties.

Technically superb, the fan is delicately detailed, from the birds in the surrounding gilt ornament to the border of painted pearls and the musical trophies on the sticks. The wavy lines decorating the exposed ribs on the reverse are probably a deliberate archaism.[1]

1. See *Allegory of Death* (cat. no. 28) and *Robert Walpole's Excise Tax* (cat. no. 27).

Exhibitions
Fans from the Oldham Collection, Museum of Fine Arts, Boston, November 25, 1977 - March 5, 1978.

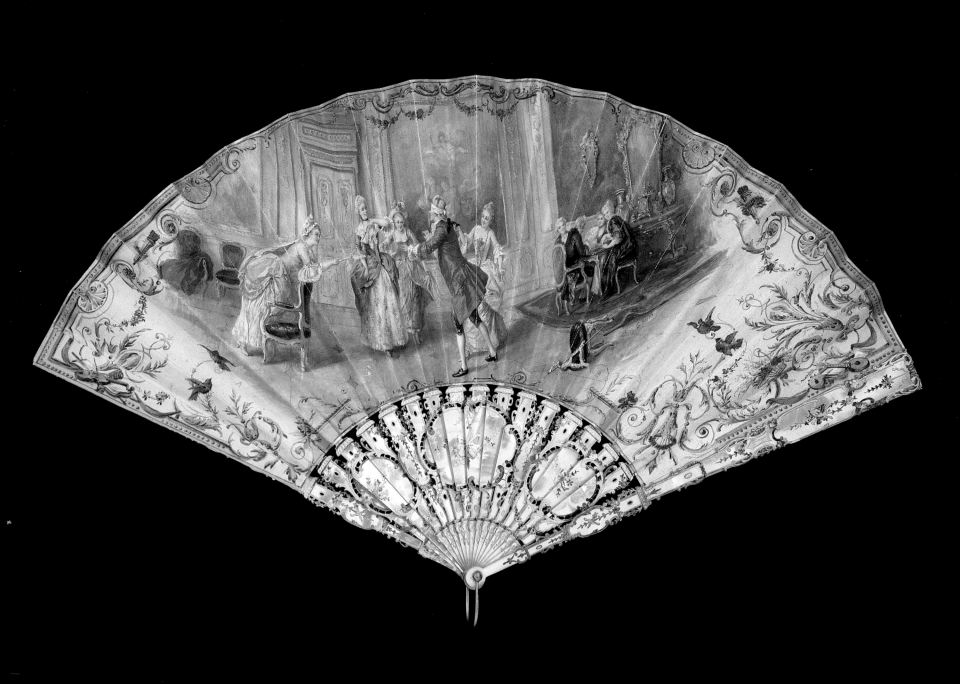

Woodland Scenes *(cat. 80)*

France, 1883-85
Skin leaf (double), painted in gouache, signed "A. DeLuc"
14 mother-of-pearl sticks, carved, painted, and varnished
Guard: 29 cm. Maximum open: 55 cm. Arc: 160° Acc. no. 1976.263

Sunlight seems to illuminate the three quiet vignettes depicted on this fan leaf. The two lateral scenes are set in the mid-eighteenth century. At left, a young woman with a distaff and spindle tries to mind her spinning as she listens to her suitor (a theme used by the American painter Thomas Eakins [1844-1916]). At right, a young woman fishes while her companion looks on. In the center, two contemporary women, protected from the sunlight by hats and a parasol, hold up their heavy skirts as they make their way through a flowering meadow. Small trees and foliage give the three scenes a natural separation.

The mother-of-pearl sticks are heavily painted with images of ducks and a greyhound in an emblazoned blanket. On the reverse, a large blank medallion hangs above another woodland meadow. It may have been intended for some kind of personalization, perhaps a portrait or a monogram. The fan has a trompe l'oeil border of pearls and is signed (*lower right, obverse*).

The fan was produced during the period of the great Impressionist painters, and it shares their interest in the effects of light. The retrospective scenes express the nostalgia that permeated the century.

IX Lace Fans

The delicacy and romantic associations of lace made it a natural choice for wedding fans and for the extravagant fans carried by women in full evening dress. A chronological review of the Museum of Fine Art's lace fans would present a pageant of changing taste in laces, from the grand church point d'Argentan, through the graceful Alençon and Duchesse, to fine Chantilly strewn with Empress Eugénie's favorite field flowers.

Ivory guard stick, (cat. 81)
France, c. 1775
1976.181

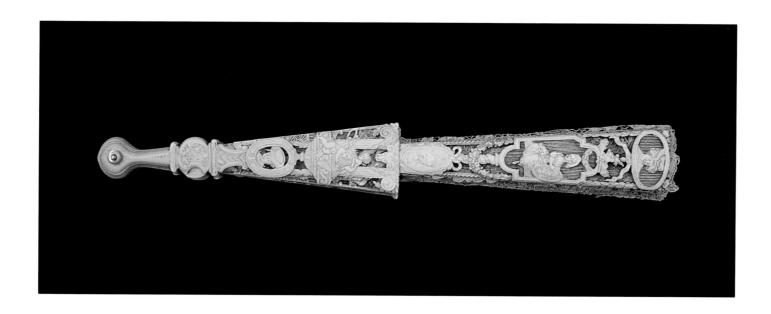

Wedding Fan *(cat. 81)*

France, c. 1775
Leaf: point d'Argentan lace
12 ivory sticks, elaborately carved
Mother-of-pearl washer on brass rivet
Guard: 28 cm. Maximum open: 54 cm. Arc: 170° Acc. no. 1976.181

This wedding fan, believed to have belonged to a princess of the house of Orléans,[1] was made at a time when eighteenth-century costumes and accessories reached their most extravagant form. Argentan lace, made entirely with a needle and once used for the albs of great prelates, is characterized by a large mesh, each hexagonal side of which has been closely worked with a buttonhole stitch. In this case, many pieces of different sizes were joined together for the leaf, resulting in some asymmetry in the design.[2]

The sticks are carved to form large medallions. When the fan is open, these show couples singing and dancing, vases, and cupids. On the obverse are various pastoral motifs and a medallion portrait of a Chinese (replaced on the reverse guard by pierced hearts).

1. See Esther Oldham, "Sheer Beauty: Early Lace Fans," *Antiques* (August 1962): 164.

2. Since the lace leaf is pieced, it is unlikely that it was produced for royalty. When lace was made for so-called royal fans in the eighteenth century, it was standard procedure to incorporate initials and a coat of arms into the design.

Provenance: DeWitt Clinton Cohen

Exhibitions

Fans from the Oldham Collection, Museum of Fine Arts, Boston, November 25, 1977 - March 5, 1978.

Publications

Encyclopaedia Britannica, s.v. "fan," plate II, no. 4.

"An Exhibition of Historic Laces and Jewels," *Bulletin of the Needle and Bobbin Club* 9, no. 2 (1924): 18, ill.

Esther Oldham. "Sheer Beauty: Early Lace Fans," *Antiques* (August 1962): 161-64, ill.

——, "Wedding and Betrothal Fans," in Fan Guild of Boston, *Fan Leaves* (Boston, 1961), VII, pp. 10-11, ill.

——, "Wedding and Betrothal Fans – 'Love and Marriage Go Together,' " *The Antiques Journal* (October 1959): 20, ill.

Esther Singleton, "The Fans of the Old Aristocracy," *International Studio* (May 1926): 42.

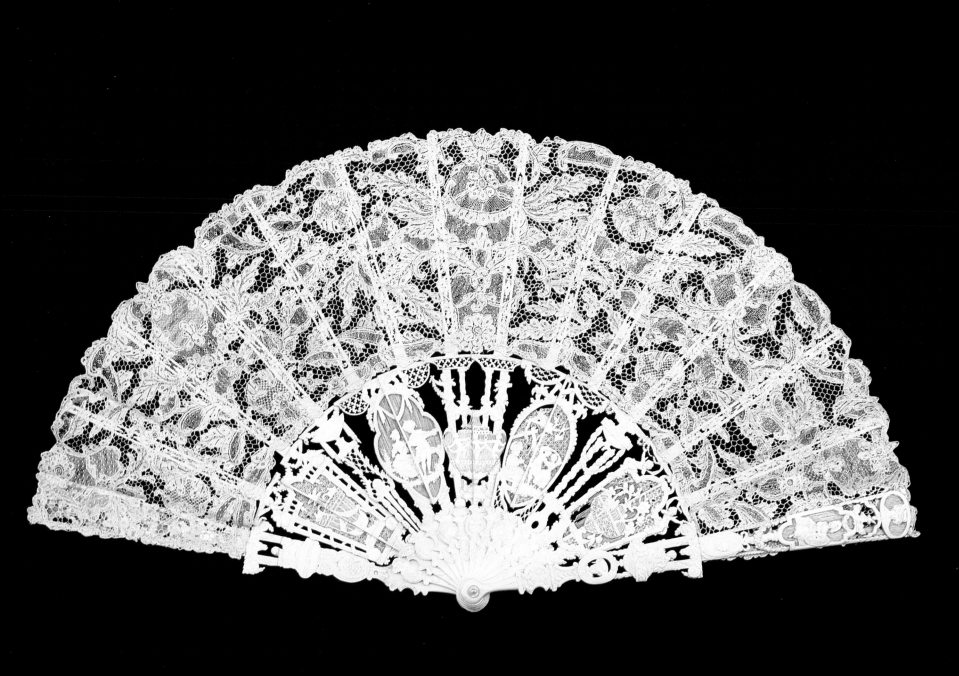

Lace Pastoral *(cat. 82)*

Belgium or England, 1770s
Leaf: point d'Angleterre lace
16 ivory sticks, pierced and carved
Diamond paste studs at rivet
Guard: 27 cm. Maximum open: 47 cm. Arc: 120° Acc. no. 1976.543

The Arcadian dream of the simple life is expressed here in a very fine and labor-intensive lace made of incredibly thin linen thread with bobbins on a pillow. In the eighteenth century, the ground used in the fabled point d'Angleterre was the *vrai droschel*, a six-sided mesh with two sides braided and the two above and two below twisted.[1]

The lace shepherd on the leaf who blows his pastoral pipe is followed by a dancing dog; the lace shepherdess, wearing an apron and a straw hat, carries a branch and leads a larger dog on a leash. The fine net (*réseau*) around them is filled with surprises such as a bow, arrow, and quiver, set off by reserves with exquisite fillings.

Teasing *putti* are carved on the sticks. Against a ribbed background, a boy with a stick over his shoulder heads the guard.

Although some point d'Angleterre lace was made in England, as the name implies, the finest came from Flanders. Supposedly, its name facilitated its being smuggled into England, since that country had established severe protective laws to encourage its own lace industry.[2]

1. See Marian Powys, *Lace and Lace-making* (Boston, 1953), p. 206.
2. Ibid., p. 25.

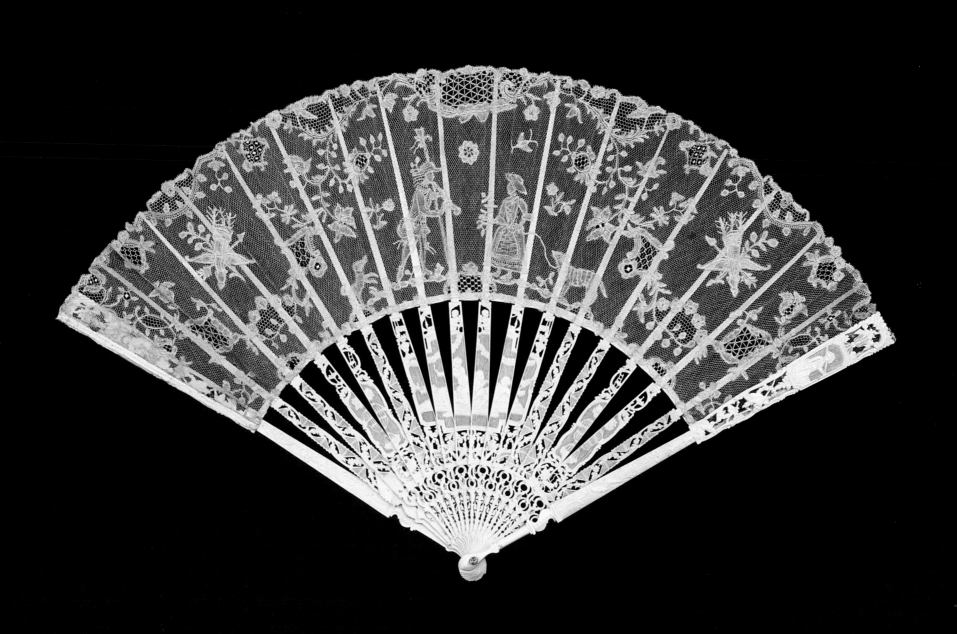

Sincerity (cat. 83)

England or France, 1790-1810
Leaf: Mechlin lace (Flanders)
22 ivory sticks, delicately pierced, ribbed, and painted in oil (?)
Diamond paste studs at rivet, large brass ring
Guard: 28.5 cm. Maximum open: 50 cm. Arc: 130° Acc. no. 1978.131
Gift of Misses Aimée and Rosamond Lamb

A bouquet of flowers surrounded by a wreath and lateral swirls is the decoration of this Mechlin lace leaf. The stiffened lace was glued and sewn to the pierced ivory ribs that support it. The beautiful sticks, probably carved in China, have flowers, birds, butterflies, and bats (for good luck), interrupted by three oval plaques, painted on both sides.

The central obverse plaque shows a scene with a man and two seated ladies dressed in costumes from the second half of the eighteenth-century. The lateral ovals are very much in the Romantic manner. All have simulated gold frames. The mood is consistently Romantic, the central oval by virtue of being retrospective, the others by an expression of a communion with nature. The inscription below the plaques reads *"Sincerité est rare."* Although the inscription is in French, it seems unlikely that France would have produced a fan of such quality at this period. England had good access to Chinese sticks, and many English fans are so provided.[1]

1. Chinese fans with ribbed ground and overall floral motif in the Museum collection are: 1976.397, 1976.400, and 1976.401.

Silk and Lace (cat. 84)

France or Belgium, 1870s
Leaf: Duchesse and point de Gaze lace with silk cartouches painted
in gouache backed with gauze, signed "Jolivet"
14 mother-of-pearl overlapping sticks, pierced and incised, with
pierced ivory ribs; guards serrated above shoulder
Mother-of-pearl button at rivet with brass ring and tassel loop
Guard: 30 cm. Maximum open: 56.5 cm. Arc: 165° Acc. no. 1976.540

A large vignette centered on a lace field is painted on silk
in pastel colors, showing three draped cherubs playing
with blue butterflies and roses. The lateral vignettes show
a landscape with poplar trees (*left*) and a crescent of roses
with a red butterfly (*right*).

The Duchesse lace that surrounds the paintings was
made on a flat, round pillow, which the lace-maker turned
with the movement of the bobbins. The flowers were
made individually and joined by little bars called *brides*.
Some of the open spaces were filled with needle lace.

The materials, decoration, and mood of the fan make it
the perfect wedding accessory.

Provenance: Mrs. Edward F. Timmins

Publications

Esther Oldham, "The Lacemaker's Art on Antique Fans," *Antiques Journal*
(June 1963), 26, ill.

——, "Wedding and Betrothal Fans," in Fan Guild of Boston, *Fans Leaves*,
(Boston, 1961), VII, p. 4, ill.

——, "Wedding and Betrothal Fans: 'Love and Marriage Go Together,' "
Antiques Journal (July 1959), 33, ill.

Lace Chinoiserie *(cat. 85)*

France, 1850-75
Leaf: black Chantilly lace
16 tortoiseshell sticks, pierced ribs
Brown painted button at rivet, tortoiseshell ring
Guard: 33 cm. Maximum open: 63 cm. Arc: 175° Acc. no. 1977.166

A chinoiserie design is carried out in very fine black silk Chantilly lace. A peacock and an urn surmount the steps of a curved Chinese bridge in a garden with flowers, rococo shapes, and an insubstantial gazebo. Elaborate pictorial designs could be executed in Chantilly lace because of its heavy outline thread. Chantilly was first made at the town of that name, but major centers for it in the nineteenth century were Grammont and Enghien in Belgium, and Bayeux and Caen in France.[1]

The fashion for black lace was probably fueled by the tastes and Spanish background of Empress Eugénie. Dresses were trimmed with Chantilly and it was used for exquisite parasol covers, mantillas, and fans.[2]

1. The black silk lace was made on a pillow with bobbins. The background of Chantilly lace is characterized by a hexagonal pattern. The designs are executed with half stitches and are filled with honeycomb, called *fond de mariage* in French.

2. A Chantilly fan with a similar chinoiserie peacock is illustrated in Nancy Armstrong, *A Collector's History of Fans* (London, 1974), title page. A Chantilly fan with a nonpictorial design is shown in the Appendix, 1976.528.

X Brisé Fans

Brisé fans, descendants of the Japanese *hiogi*, were inspired more directly by the Chinese export fans that served as their immediate models. In use, they are heavier to handle than fans with skin or paper leaves, but they display to advantage such rich materials as ivory, silver filigree, and tortoiseshell. Those of uncarved ivory offered artists a flat surface for decoration.

Typical examples from China are the exquisite tortoise-shell (cat. no. 25) and the delicately carved ivory (1976.402, Appendix). Western fan-makers added such un-Chinese developments as high-relief carving (cat. no. 88), steel piqué (43.2086, Appendix) and even jeweled guards (1976.339, Appendix).

Ivory guard stick, jeweled
Russia(?), 1830-55
1976.339, (Appendix)

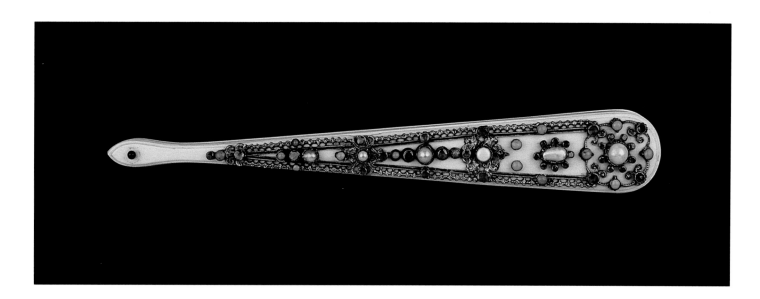

Couple in Landscape (cat. 86)

Netherlands, 1700-30
Brisé fan, 23 bone blades, painted in tempera, at least one missing
Guard: 21 cm. Maximum open: 33 cm. Arc: 120° Acc. 52.1323
Gift of Miss Elizabeth G. Norton

Brilliant color and a chintzlike background distinguish this early-eighteenth-century Dutch brisé fan. Made of bone rather than ivory, and painted in tempera instead of oils, the fan also lacks the usual lustrous varnished surface. Costume details of the seated couple confirm the date. The heart-shaped reserves in blue and rose are architectural in subject and painted *en camaïeu*, that is, in shades of one color, a style popular at the time. The chinoiserie scene on the sticks is also early in style.

In the seventeenth century, Dutch traders became involved in the production and trading of the painted cottons of India, originally as barter to secure precious spices from the Spice Islands. By the mid-seventeenth century, however, the trade in these hand-painted and dyed chintzes rivaled that of spices. Twenty-six days were required to produce these "flowery fantasies," using mordant and resist techniques and drawing inspiration from brocaded silks, English crewel, and French block prints. They were styled for export to Holland, England, and France.[1]

1. See Alice Baldwin Beer, *Trade Goods: A Study of Indian Chintz* (Washington, D.C., 1970): pp. 15-19, 29-30.

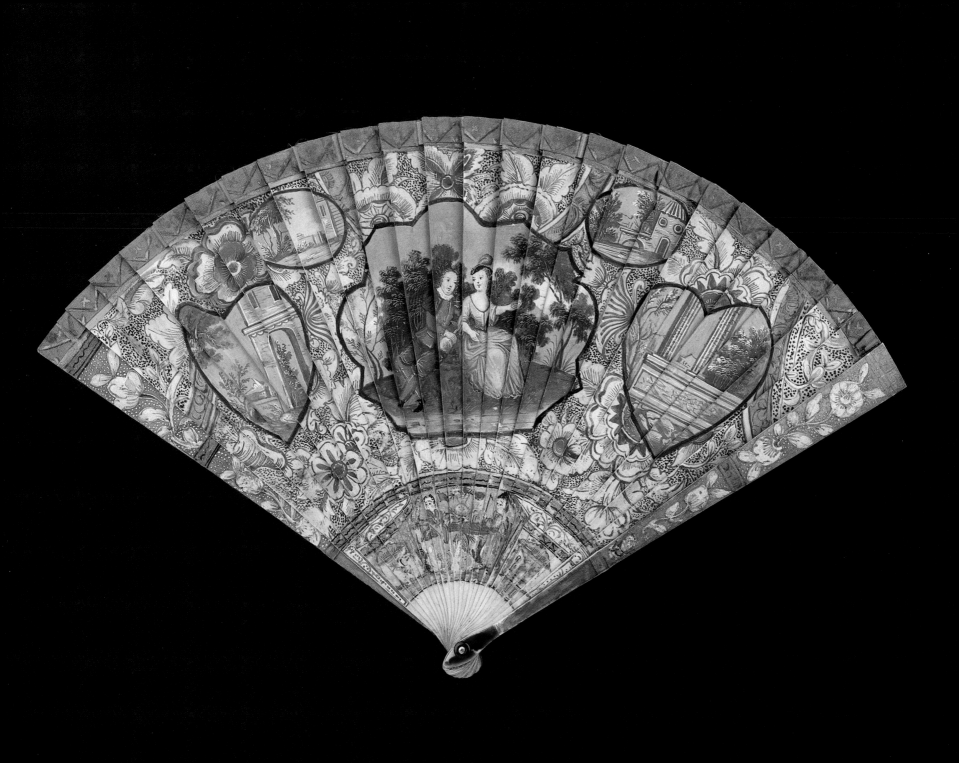

Silver Filigree, "M.L.B." *(cat. 87)*

Italy(?), 1810-30
Brisé fan, 14 silver filigree blades with gray silk connecting ribbon
Silver washer and filigree ring
Guard: 20 cm. Maximum open: 36.5 cm. Arc: 145° Acc. no. 1976.354

This nonfunctional but extremely ornamental fan was made of fine silver wire, soldered together in an intricate design that incorporates such motifs as the stylized lily, or fleur-de-lis, the rose, the heart, and, by a stretch of the imagination, the star. The ring, which would have been unusual at the time of manufacture, may be a later addition.[1]

According to documentation received with the fan, it belonged to Marie Louise (1791-1847), daughter of the Austrian emperor Francis I. She became the second wife of Napoleon I in 1810. When Napoleon was forced to abdicate in 1814, the allied powers at the Congress of Vienna gave Marie Louise and her son the duchy of Parma. In 1844, when the duchess lost her state, the fan went to Professor Gondenzi of Bologna for his Napoleonic museum. Gondenzi gave the fan to a Professor Casale of Venice in 1860 on the occasion of his marriage. Contessa Antoinette Zuppiani of Asolo bought the fan from Professor Casale, and her account of the fan's provenance was signed, stamped, and witnessed in 1921. The original maroon leather box has survived, stamped in gold with a crown and the initials "M.L.B."

1. A very similar fan is in the Mrs. Walter G. Nord Collection at the Western Reserve Historical Society, Cleveland, Ohio.

Provenance: Professor Gondenzi, 1844; Professor Casale, 1860; Contessa Antoinette Zuppiani; Pauline H. Shirer; Surradge R. Cameron.

Publications
Esther Oldham, "Fans of the Napoleonic Era," *Antiques* (January 1970): 135-39, fig. 9.
Walter A. Dyer, "An Instrument Used by Ladies," *Antiques* (January 1925): 20-25, fig. 8.

Ivory Wheat *(cat. 88)*

Germany, c. 1875
Brisé fan, 19 ivory blades with white silk connecting ribbon
Heavy guards carved in high relief
Long ivory chain and chatelaine attachment
Guard: 19.5 cm. Maximum open: 33 cm. Arc: 165° Acc. no. 51.2002
Gift of Miss Frances Fowler and Professor Harold North Fowler

The guards of this heavy brisé fan were carved to resemble a sheaf of wheat tied with a ribbon, and the inner blades were shaped to conform with this image in a closed position. The round chatelaine attachment for the belt also resembles a sheaf of wheat, with the addition of roses, forget-me-nots, and lilies of the valley. The ivory chain hooks onto a ring at the fan's base. Two other brisé fans in the collection feature roses instead of wheat (1976.338 and 50.3163).[1]

1. Both wheat and rose examples, nearly identical to the Boston fans, were illustrated in Bertha de Vere Green, *A Collector's Guide to Fans Over the Ages* (London, 1975), p. 256 ff, fig. 38, and described as "English, c. 1830-40."

Tortoiseshell Fontange (cat. 89)

Europe, 1905-10
Brisé fan, 16 tortoiseshell blades with ring at rivet
Maroon silk connecting ribbon, cord, loop, and tassel
Guard: 16.4 cm. Maximum open: 30 cm. Arc: 170° Acc. no. 43.1299
Elizabeth Day McCormick Collection

The substitutes developed during the nineteenth century to imitate tortoiseshell were so successful that it is difficult to distinguish the true tortoiseshell, used in this fan, from its impersonators. Protein material from horns or hoofs, processed with heat, was pressed or cast, then given characteristic tortoiseshell markings with chemicals. A microscope is almost a necessity in assessing shell authenticity. An examination of transitions from dark to light in the markings is useful in identifying the imitation.

Pigmentation in the true shell, as in the present example, penetrates the entire depth of the sample, subtly dispersed; in an imitation, the pigmentation appears more like a liquid applied to the surface. The graceful fontange shape, popular at the end of the century and the beginning of the new era, exploits the translucent beauty of the material.[1]

1. The fontange shape is explained in connection with cat. no. 99, note 1.

XI New Forms and Functions

Throughout the nineteenth century, the relation between costume and fan grew increasingly close. Silks and satins, sequins and feathers, began to rival pictorial subjects on fan leaves. The slim gowns of the First Empire eliminated the separate pockets formerly worn under skirts. Women carried fans, many of them made of horn, which were small enough to fit into reticules, like the "imperceptible" fan (43.2092, Appendix). Others were fitted with lorgnette lenses for opera-goers (cat. nos. 92 and 93).

Fans assumed new roles along with new shapes. At mid-century they doubled as *parasolettes* and, occasionally, as *carnets de bal* (1976.254 and 1976.256, Appendix). One innovative type was hinged to bend double (1976.261, Appendix); another folded into a guitar-shaped case (1976.262, Appendix). Yankee ingenuity designed one to fit into a man's pocket (1976.376, Appendix).

The upholstered ladies of the 1870s wore hats trimmed with whole birds and carried fans similarly provisioned (63.663, Appendix). Women and fans of the 1890s were growing bolder (see 1976.516, Appendix). In the 1920s, a woman was assured a grand entrance if she carried an electrifying fan like *Tiger Feathers* (cat. no. 100).

Wood guard stick with gold leaf, (cat. 94)
United States (Massachusetts), 1867-70
1976.361

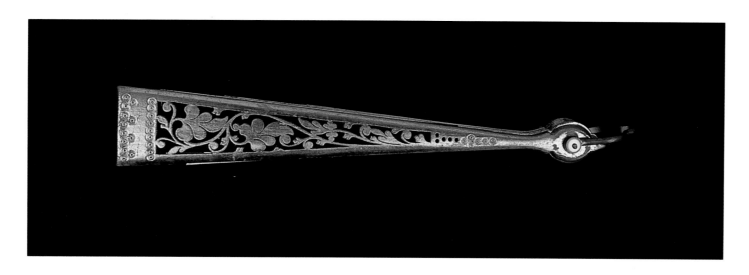

Decorative Bands (cat. 90)

France or England, 1795-99
White striped silk leaf (double), bands painted in gouache, applied sequins and brass- and silver-plated copper spangles
18 bone sticks, pierced; guards with applied steel "pearls" and plaques
Guard: 25 cm. Maximum open: 45 cm. Arc: 135° Acc. no. 1976.243

The bone sticks are pierced in motifs that could be interpreted as classical: possibly laurel wreaths and wheat. The deepening width of the leaf in relation to the sticks marks the fan as transitional between the type common during the Revolutionary period and that typical of the First Empire.

The leaf is painted in decorative bands of spiraling vines and swags, ornamented with fine gold lines, brass, and gilt spangles. Star-shaped spangles are used with the sequins.

The fan's effect is fresh and pretty, well suited to the thin, unstructured dresses of the period.

Empire Belle (cat. 91)

France(?), 1805-10
Bluish-white silk leaf (single), painted in watercolor and embroidered with silver-plated copper sequins; applied ivory
14 short mother-of-pearl sticks, incised, with piqué work and applied silver
Diamond paste studs at rivet
Guard: 21.5 cm. Maximum open: 37.5 cm.   Arc: 135° Acc. no. 65.500
Gift of Mrs. Charles C. Cabot in memory of Mrs. Charles J. White

The fragile silk leaf, deep in proportion to the sticks and weighted with many small steel sequins, has suffered predictable losses. It has been faithfully, if not always skillfully, repaired over the years. One can still admire the charming scene, depicting a fashionable lady of the First Empire in a lavender bonnet, gloves, and flat slippers, and holding a mandolin. The skirt of her high-waisted gown is entirely covered with small sequins, and they also form heavy swags above her head. The remarkable condition of her face is explained by the fact that it is made of ivory, painted and applied to the silk, in the manner of the so-called "Mandarin" fans exported from China (see cat. no. 26).

Another fan in the collection, illustrated in the Appendix (43.2098), shows the close relationship of dress and accessory in the First Empire period.

"Love's Arrows" Lorgnette (cat. 92)

France or Netherlands, c. 1790
Brisé fan, 17 arrow-shaped horn blades, pierced and gilded; guards double thickness to accommodate lens set near top
White silk connecting ribbon
Horn button at rivet
Guard: 15 cm. Maximum open: 127 cm. Arc: 150° Acc. no. 43.2086
Elizabeth Day McCormick Collection

The serrated blades have stars at their heads, arrows at their bases. Gilt-silver foil has been applied for decoration, with inset steel piqué and rings around the circular peepholes.[1]

Lorgnette fans like this one were small enough to fit into a reticule, making them useful at the theater or opera.

1. Another "Love's Arrows" lorgnette fan (Rosse-Messel Collection) was illustrated by Nancy Armstrong in *Fans from the Fitzwilliam* (Cambridge, 1985), no. 20.

"Cockade" Lorgnette (cat. 93)

France, c. 1800
Brisé fan, 19 horn blades, pierced, decorated with gilt-silver and piqué work
Connecting white twill silk ribbon, blue flowers painted in watercolor
Opera-glass magnifier set in center at rivet
Guard: 16.5 cm. Diameter: 17.5 cm. Acc. no. 43.2084
Elizabeth Day McCormick Collection

The horn blades of this circular brisé fan are delicately pierced and decorated with gilt-silver pyramid and leaf shapes. The guards extend to form handles ending in rings to hold the fan open. The outer edge is crenellated.

An interesting comparison can be made between this fan and a similar Chinese export fan carved in ivory, from about the same period (1976.396). The Chinese export fan has no opera-glass feature.

Black and Gold (cat. 94)

United States (Weymouth, Mass.)
Edmund Soper Hunt Fan Factory, 1867-70
Black silk leaf (double), with black tape binding
18 pierced wood sticks, covered with gold leaf
Mother-of-pearl washers at rivet, brass ring
Guard: 21 cm. Maximum open: 37.5 cm. Arc: 160° Acc. no. 1976.361

The leaf of this bold fan was cut of plain black silk to fit the bracket shape formed by the sticks when fully open. The sticks, of different length, were covered with gold leaf, a specialty of the Hunt fan factory.[1] Edmund Soper Hunt employed many men and women in his factory, although the women were particularly expert in applying the gilding directly to the wooden sticks without any undercoating of gesso or bole. The effect is rather modern and flashy.

The same gold leaf is used with purple satin and sequins in another fan in the collection (1976.362, Appendix).

1. Edmund Soper Hunt continued making fans in Weymouth until 1876, when his brother, Fred Hunt, and Frank Allen took over the factory.

Provenance: Mrs. Edna L. Frye

Exhibition
Fans From the Oldham Collection, Museum of Fine Arts, Boston, November 25,1977-March 5, 1978.

Publications
Celebration of Esther Oldham: A Tribute to a Beloved Patron of Fans, The Fan Association of North America (Boston, 1985), p. 23.

Esther Oldham, "America's First Fan Factory," part 1, *Spinning Wheel* (January-February 1972): 62-64.

Luna Moth (cat. 95)

United States (East Braintree, Mass.), c. 1890
Allen Fan Company
Painted by George Keiswetter
White silk leaf (single), painted in oil(?); applied brass, plated steel, silver-plated copper sequins, gilt-silver threads, and net
13 wood sticks (hornbeam?), carved and painted green, silver, and gilt-silver
Guard : 37 cm. Maximum open: 66 cm. Arc: 160° Acc. no. 1976.369

George Keiswetter, chief painter at the Allen Fan Company, which was located in East Braintree from 1880 to 1899,[1] specialized in painting birds and insects.[2] Keiswetter's imagination and artistry were nowhere more successful than in this adaptation of the form and coloration of the large American luna moth (*tropaea luna*) to the format of the folding fan.

The delicate green anterior wings, swept forward for the leaf, are separated by an insert of gold mesh. They bear the moth's characteristic spots surrounded by rings of light yellow, blue, and black. The leaf sparkles with colored and metallic sequins and gilt-silver thread. The form of the moth's body serves as the central stick. Lateral supporting sticks are mounted on the outside of the leaf, contributing to the grace and movement of the design. The fan's theatricality and innovative spirit anticipated by two decades the fans of the new century.

1. In 1885, the Allen Fan Company was established by Frank B. Allen in one of the buildings of the Jenkins Manufacturing Company in East Braintree, Massachusetts, where it operated until 1899. Following the death of Allen in April of 1899, the fan works was operated by Ignatz Strauss of New York City, and was known locally as the Strauss Fan Factory. Strauss moved the business to New York in June of 1901. The author is grateful to Barbara M. Delorey, curator of the Braintree Historical Society for information on the Hunt-Allen fan companies. Mrs. Delorey is preparing a manuscript on the subject.

2. George Keiswetter, a gifted artist and fine musician, emigrated from Breslau, Germany (now Wroclaw, Poland). Grace E. A. Ford, who later became Mrs. George Keiswetter, was one of the most accomplished woman fan painters as well as a prolific commercial artist.

Exhibitions

Fans from the Oldham Collection, Museum of Fine Arts, Boston, November 25, 1977 - March 5, 1978.

Publications

Celebration of Esther Oldham: A Tribute to a Beloved Patron of Fans, The Fan Association of North America (Boston, 1985), p. 24.

Esther Oldham, "America's First Fan Factory," part 2, *Spinning Wheel* (March 1972): 8-10.

Ostrich Feathers *(cat. 96)*

Europe, 1880s
Feather brisé, natural ostrich feathers
16 dark faux tortoiseshell blades
Guard: 39 cm. Maximum open: 71 cm. Arc: 170° Acc. no. 1976.510

The majesty of ostrich plumes made them a traditional accessory of royalty throughout history. King Tutankhamun and Queen Elizabeth I both carried rigid fans made of the plumes. In 1981, three ostrich feathers formed the fixed "leaf" of the fan commemorating the marriage of Charles, Prince of Wales, and Lady Diana Spencer (1982.451, Appendix).[1]

In the last two decades of the nineteenth century, folding fans of ostrich plumes were the classic evening accessory. White plumes were often mounted on iridescent mother-of-pearl sticks; black plumes were sometimes enhanced by diamond-studded guards.

The process of "stripping" adds interest to the surface of the present example. The lower feathers of selected plumes were removed, leaving only a tuft of feathers near the very end. These tiny tufts respond to the slightest air current, keeping the surface in almost constant motion.

1. The fan's design duplicated the insignia of the Prince of Wales.

African Starling (cat. 97)

Europe, 1880-1900
Feather brisé, African starling and hummingbird feathers
16 dark faux tortoiseshell blades; ring for brown silk loop and tassel
Brown silk connecting ribbon
Guard: 20 cm. Maximum open: 44 cm. Arc: 155° Acc. no. 1976.514

The successful use of feathers for fan production came after 1865, when ostriches were domesticated in the Cape colony of South Africa. There was a subsequent attempt to raise even more exotic, brilliantly colored species in western Europe, which had some success. These "feathers of fantasy," as they were called, could be gathered at moulting time without sacrificing the birds.[1]

In the present example, royal blue and magenta feathers from the African starling (*Laphophore*) were glued to a support of ordinary domestic feathers, probably duck. Over the years, the domestic feathers have proved particularly susceptible to insect attack and suffered seriously.

The design of a rose with buds and leaves on the left side was made by applying tiny hummingbird feathers.

1. See Musée de la Mode et du Costume, *L'Eventail: Miroir de la Belle Epoque* (Paris, 1985), p. 67.

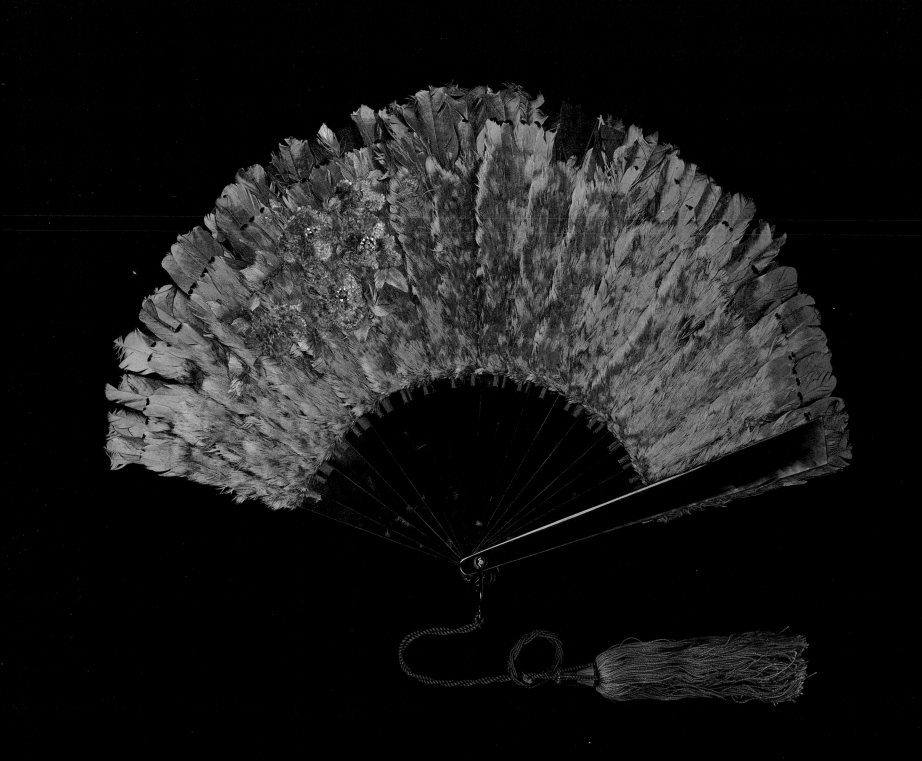

The Swan (cat. 98)

France, c. 1905
White silk satin leaf (double), painted in watercolor and embroidered with sequins
10 plain ivory sticks
Steel button and ring at rivet
Guard: 24 cm. Maximum open: 42.5 cm. Arc: 160° Acc. no. 53.2179
Gift of Mr. H. Wade White

The bold curve of the swan's neck dominates the leaf's design. Her wings spread out to fill the leaf, the top edge discreetly scalloped to give the effect of feathers. Sequins accent the line where the gray water meets the swan's body, and the sequins are repeated below to suggest ripples.

The straight-fronted corsets worn by women in the early years of the century made them very long-waisted and bent their bodies into a swayed, swanlike posture.

This fan served as the perfect complement to the shape then in fashion.

Another elegant swan is seen in the foreground of the *Pastoral Reprise* fan (cat. no. 78) and was the feature of a signed fan of the period designed by A. Thomasse for Duvelleroy.[1]

1. See Musée de la Mode et du Costume, *L'Eventail: Miroir de la Belle Epoque* (Paris, 1985), p. 51, fig. 30, cat. no. 28.

Gold Fontange *(cat. 99)*

France, c. 1905
Leaf of silver-plated copper threads, applied brass sequins and silver-plated copper metal forms
12 bone sticks, pierced and gilded, with "gold" piqué work
Guards and sticks: 15-22 cm. Maximum open: 25 cm. Arc: 140°
Acc. no. 1986.490
Gift of Mrs. Robert Lee Wolff in memory of Rosamond Capen Andrews (Mrs. Oliver Andrews)

The shape of the leaf has been likened to the late-seventeenth-century headdress called the *fontange* after a mademoiselle favored by Louis XIV.[1] Typically in fans of this type, the leaf is deepest at midpoint, narrowing to the short guard sticks. Silver-plated copper thread (on a silk core) was used variously as an element in the gauze weave, as lace, and as embroidery.[2] Brass and gilt sequins and spangles, both smooth and textured, are attached, together with hollow metal forms in diamond and insect-wing shapes.

The metal used resulted in a fan that is very heavy for its size.

The short bone sticks are machine carved and pierced, then painted with gilt paint. Considerable gold piqué work is missing.

1. According to the story, Mlle de Fontanges bound up her hair with a ribbon while hunting with the king, producing an effect that pleased the monarch and started a fashion.

2. Gold net and gold lace figured prominently in the designs of Callot Soeurs, the notable Parisian couturières of the period.

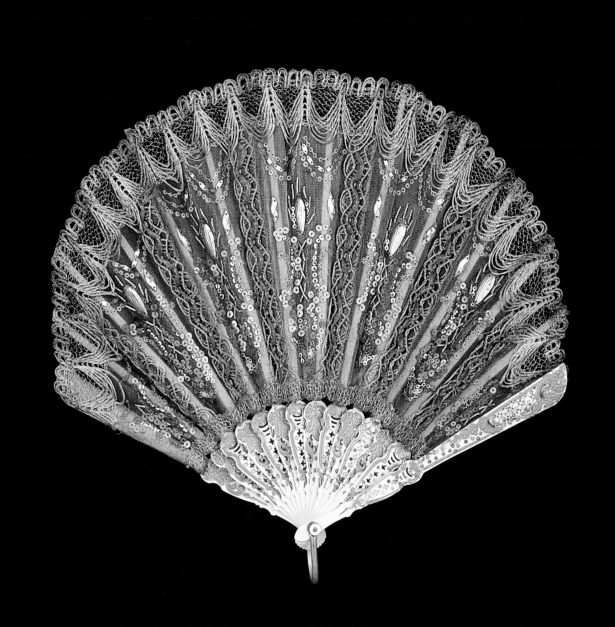

Tiger Feathers *(cat. 100)*

France, 1915-25
Feather brisé, sharply pointed dyed orange feathers
16 dark reformed protein blades
Guard: 23 cm. Feathers: 25-47 cm. Maximum open: 56 cm.
Acc. no. 50.3166
Gift of Mrs. J.D. Cameron Bradley

This striking fan recalls the *fontange* in its arrangement of feathers, ascending in order of height toward the center. The color, feather shape, and irregular markings produce a flamelike effect that is highly theatrical. The orange shade, popular in the 1920s, was known as "Tango."

APPENDIX I

Forty-five Fans in Small Format

01.6688

43.2080

17.1680

43.2082

43.1293

43.2092

01.6688   France, 1750s   *The Kite*
The double paper leaf is painted in gouache. Sticks are of ivory, pierced and painted. In contrast to the pastoral make-believe scenes on many fans, the young people depicted here are enjoying the most innocent and unpretentious of country pleasures.
Bequest of Mrs. Arthur Croft

17.1680   England, 1740s   *Green Garland Sticks*
The single skin leaf is painted in gouache. Green garlands, painted in green, black, and gold, decorate the ivory sticks. The shepherd and shepherdess of the pastoral scene are provided with crooks.
Gift of Miss Sarah Dearborn

43.1293   Spain, 1850s   *Spanish Pastoral*
The narrow paper leaf, lithographed and painted, rests on wood sticks. A pastoral scene of adults in "Renaissance" costumes with children and a dog are flanked by lateral sections of blue-violet shiny paper, embossed and gilded.
Elizabeth Day McCormick Collection

43.2080   England, 1795-1800   *Mythological Group*
Bits of mica or mother-of-pearl decorate the painted paper leaf above carved ivory sticks, which are probably Chinese. Under a burst of radiating light, robed figures with joined hands dance under a swag border. Painted in the style of William Marshall Craig, court painter to Queen Charlotte Sophia, wife of George III.
Elizabeth Day McCormick Collection

43.2082   *Garden Scene*
China, for export, 1750-1800
The internal evidence for the dating of this ivory brisé fan is contradictory. The very long coats of the men suggest an early date, but the rendering of flowers and other details resembles that found on porcelains of the second half of the century. Nancy Armstrong (*A Collector's History of Fans* [London, 1974], p. 164) illustrated a fan with similar piercing, dating it first quarter of the eighteenth century.
Elizabeth Day McCormick Collection

43.2092   France, 1800-25   *Imperceptible*
The guard blades of this tiny horn fan measure only 9.5 cm. (3 3/4 in.). The blades are decorated with steel piqué work.
Elizabeth Day McCormick Collection

43.2095

47.1528

43.2098

63.663

46.318

1976.184

43.2095   France(?), 1830-35   *Tall Crockets*
Horn brisé blades, pierced and gilded at the top, are
painted with medallions of classical and contemporary
figures. The guards are of stamped brass.
Elizabeth Day McCormick Collection

43.2098   France or England,   *Empire Net*
1800-30
Forms of cut steel and tinted foil provide glittering decoration for this leaf of white net. The embroidery, done
with black thread, is typical of this kind of fan. The sticks
are of horn.
Elizabeth Day McCormick Collection

46.318   England, 1730-50   *The Pannier*
A country scene is painted in gouache on the single skin
leaf. A woman wearing a large pannier stands on the
stairs of a country house under a prominent floral border. The ivory sticks were pierced, painted, and partially
varnished. Their motifs point to a common provenance
with the *Mask Fan* (cat. no. 54).
Miss Amelia Peabody and Mr. William S. Eaton

47.1528   France, c. 1875   *Red Leather Cockade*
A circular leaf of pleated red silk makes a cockade form
when extended. When not in use, it folds into a handle of
gold-tooled red leather.
Gift of Miss Marion C. Tripp

63.663   France(?), 1870s   *Pink Feather Screen*
White down surrounds a fixed fan leaf of pale pink
feathers on which orange blossoms made of feathers and
a stuffed hummingbird are arranged. The type seems to
have originated in Brazil, but examples are known from
as far distant as Canada.
Gift of Mrs. Yves Henry Buhler

1976.184   Netherlands, 1745-55   *Genre Scene*
The skin leaf is painted in gouache with a scene of children playing and singing for the entertainment of their
elders. The ivory sticks have applied panels of gold and
are inlaid with mother-of-pearl and silver piqué work.

1976.189

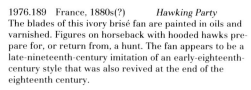

1976.189   France, 1880s(?)   *Hawking Party*
The blades of this ivory brisé fan are painted in oils and varnished. Figures on horseback with hooded hawks prepare for, or return from, a hunt. The fan appears to be a late-nineteenth-century imitation of an early-eighteenth-century style that was also revived at the end of the eighteenth century.

1976.204   *The Picnic*
Netherlands, 1735-45/1780s
The ivory blades of this brisé fan are painted in oil and partially varnished. The central scene, showing a couple enjoying a picnic meal, and the side panels are set off by pierced designs in the ivory.

1976.211   France, 1755-60   *Mourning Cabriolet*
The paper leaf, divided into two sections, was painted in gouache in tones of grisaille. Three rococo frames divide the upper leaf. The subject is a rural landscape.

1976.212   Europe, 1755-60   *Chinoiserie Cabriolet*
The printed and hand-colored paper leaf, divided into two sections, shows chinoiserie figures and a "Chinese" version of the two-wheeled cabriolet. The sticks are wood.

1976.223   England, 1740s   *Green Garden*
The paper leaf is painted in green tones (*en camaïeu*), showing a man and woman before a formal garden. The ivory sticks are painted in circle and flower motifs with extensions that give a lattice effect. A "coin" border decorates the reverse.

1976.232   France, 1783-85   *Balloons*
The silk leaf with cutouts in the shape of balloons qualifies this as a domino fan. Branches with spangled flowers and chain-stitch leaves spread out from a blue and orange receptacle holding roses. The twelve cutout shapes are spaced over the leaf to afford good viewing.

1976.204

1976.223

1976.211

1976.232

1976.212

1976.246

1976.254

1976.248

1976.256

1976.251

1976.261

1976.246   France, 1775-85   *Dominotier*
The crudely painted paper leaf on plain bone sticks is a good example of the wallpaper fan. On either side of a central oval cartouche depicting a rural couple, lateral floral sections are separated by wave and diagonal patterns.

1976.248   France, 1810-20   *Moonlight Scene*
The small brisé fan of light horn has pierced blades painted with cornucopias and a central landscape illuminated by a full moon.

1976.251   England, 1830s   *Boating Party*
The leaf (paper recto and skin verso) has been lithographed, stenciled, and touched up with gouache. Its descriptive detail of contemporary costume should make it a costume historian's delight. The bone sticks are decorated with silver leaf.

1976.254   France, 1840s   *Parasolette*
A green silk leaf opens cockade-fashion around mother-of-pearl buttons to form a carriage *parasolette*. The angle is adjusted by a silk string with tassel.

1976.256   France, 1825-30   *Souvenir*
The blades of this brisé fan are ivory, covered with skin. On the plain reverse is inscribed the names of friends and various sayings, written with a removable metal stylus inserted in a guard.

1976.261   France, c. 1866   *Folding Fan*
This fan for pocket or purse is of silk gauze covered with sequins and spangles. The hinges at the shoulder allow it to fold. Its invention was attributed by Blondel to Auguste Buinot (mid-nineteenth century).

1976.262

1976.310

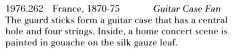

1976.262   France, 1870-75   *Guitar Case Fan*
The guard sticks form a guitar case that has a central hole and four strings. Inside, a home concert scene is painted in gouache on the silk gauze leaf.

1976.264   France, c. 1875   *Expanding Fan*
The stiff blue satin leaf, painted with pink morning glories, is not attached to the sticks at the lower edge and can, therefore, be slid down toward the rivet in a closed position, reducing the apparent length by 7.5 cm. (3 in.) from 24.5 cm. (9¾ in.) to 17 cm. (6¾ in.). This telescoping feature made the fan a convenient accessory for purse or pocket.

1976.288   Spain, c. 1880   *Cork Brisé*
The cork blades are painted with fruit, flowers, and insects, and ornament is applied to the guards.

1976.310   England, 1795   *Royal Engagement*
The paper leaf has a stipple engraving of George, Prince of Wales (later George IV) and Princess Caroline, with riddles, verses, lateral vignettes, and a top border of caricatures. It was published in January 1795 by Sudlow's Fan Warehouse.

1976.314   England, 1782   *Battle of the Saints*
The paper leaf, printed, painted, and ornamented with sequins, commemorates the sea battle off the West Indies in which Admiral Rodney was victorious over the French forces under the Comte de Grasse.

1976.330   *Royal Museum*
Germany (Berlin), 1830
The horn blades are painted and gilded with an image of the Royal Museum, now known as the "Old Museum," in Berlin. Classical ornament flanks the central scene.

1976.264

1976.314

1976.288

1976.330

254

1976.335

1976.349

1976.339

1976.351

1976.345

1976.362

1976.335   Austria (Vienna;   *Viennese Garden*
Rodeck), 1870-75
The silk leaf, painted by E. Bayard, shows four women
and a man in a garden with a bust of Pan. A silver plaque
on the reverse is inscribed "Stéphanie." The guards are
ornamented with gilt-silver, pearls, garnets, and enamel.

1976.339   Russia(?), 1830-55   *Jeweled Brisé*
The guards of this ivory brisé fan are ornamented with
gilt-silver, cut and cabochon garnets, Ural river pearls,
and turquoise. It is believed to have belonged to a grand
duchess and to have come from the czar's summer palace, Tsarskoe-Selo.

1976.345   Italy, c. 1760   *Trevi Fountain*
The skin leaf, painted in gouache, is supported on Oriental lacquered sticks. The Trevi fountain, in the central
position, is surrounded by street activity.

1976.349   Italy, 1780s   *Quirinale Palace*
The ivory sticks are pierced in a "classical" design, and
the leaf's blue-backed panels with similar motifs flank a
central scene depicting the palace, museums, and the
Trajan and Antonine columns. The original tourists'
notes on the reverse identify the monuments.

1976.351   Italy, 1830s   *Questions and
Answers*
Ivory wheels, set into the tops of the guards, activate a
conversation game in which questions and answers with
a romantic flavor are exchanged. The silk leaf is printed
and painted. The language is a Roman dialect.

1976.362   United States   *Purple with Spangles*
(Weymouth, Mass.), 1867-76
The narrow satin leaf is decorated with brass sequins
and spangles. Mechanically carved wood sticks covered
with gold leaf give a lattice effect. It was made at
Edmund Soper Hunt's fan factory.

255

1976.376

1976.516

1976.387

1976.523

1976.402

1976.528

1976.376	*Man's Folding Fan*

United States (New York), after 1888
A leaf of embossed black glazed cotton, imitating leather, folds into thirds when not in use. A sliding handle of wood, covered with the same material and provided with a top hook, secures the leaf when it is unfolded and the handle is extended. The patent was filed by Friedman Sternheimer in 1888. The slightly curved leaf is designed to fit comfortably into a man's pocket.

1976.387 Cuba (Havana), 1865 *Lincoln Commemorative*
Ornate sticks of stamped brass support a paper leaf with lithographed scenes of Lincoln's assassination (*obverse*) and the naval battle of the *Monitor* and the *Merrimac* (*reverse*). Spanish songs about the martyrdom and oval photo medallions of American generals and women of royal European families offer additional interest. It was made by Bart.^e Crespo de Borbon.

1976.402 *Ivory Brisé*
China, for export, 1790s
The pierced and carved ivory blades have a central monogram shield, heavily draped, with the initials "HP." Lateral medallions show a ship and fortress at left, a pagoda by a stream at right. The fretwork and ribbing are especially fine, with horizontal drifts of islands, boats, and pagodas. A deeply carved floral motif decorates the guards. An unusual serrated mother-of-pearl button surrounds the rivet.

1976.516 Europe, c. 1910 *Baroque Feathers*
The small red feathers of the central design were dyed several shades, then glued to the blades, probably over the curled brown feathers of domestic fowl. Seen from the back, the blades are of the *fontange* shape, with the longest blade in the center.

1976.523 France, 1760s *Binche Pastoral*
Alternating wide and narrow strips of Binche lace have been sewn together for the leaf. A vignette showing the usual pastoral couple was glued on to the lace leaf. Iridescent mother-of-pearl forms a backing for the central group of painted ivory sticks.

1976.528 Belgium, c. 1912 *Chantilly*
Interconnecting floral medallions are an unusual design for Chantilly lace. The lace is backed by white silk and supported by mother-of-pearl sticks, possibly abalone.

1982.451

1982.451   *Royal Wedding*
England (London), 1981
Three white plumes from the male ostrich, fixed on a
sterling silver handle with insignia and inscription, com-
memorate the marriage of Charles, Prince of Wales, and
Lady Diana Spencer on July 29, 1981. The fan was made
by Thomas Dobbie in association with the Fan Circle
International.

1986.485   France, 1800-1805   *Psyche Discovering*
                                     Cupid
In a room with a marble floor, Psyche, holding an oil
lamp, and her companion, dressed *à la grecque*, look
toward the sleeping Cupid. The young god rests under a
gold-fringed rose satin canopy supported by "silver" columns wound with garlands. The silk leaf was painted,
embroidered, and lavished with large and small sequins
and with applied painted ivory for the women's faces
and throats. In subject, materials, and treatment, the fan
exemplifies First Empire taste.
Gift of Rosamond Capen Wolff Purcell

1986.491   *Domino Fan*
France (Paris; Kees), c. 1890
The green silk leaf, painted and decorated with sequins
and spangles on reformed protein sticks, shows three
figures in white "eighteenth-century" costumes. Lateral
cutout sections allow the wearer the visibility to qualify it
as a domino fan.
Gift of Mrs. Robert Lee Wolff in memory of Mathilde A.
Wolff (Mrs. Samuel Lee Wolff)

1986.485

1986.491

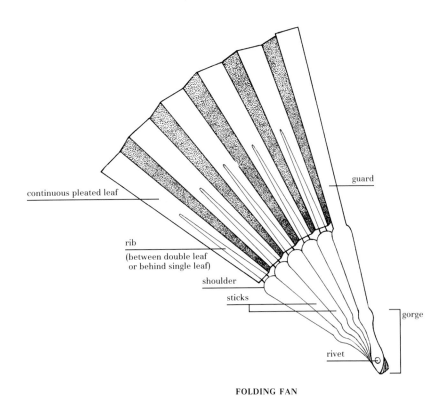

continuous pleated leaf

guard

rib
(between double leaf
or behind single leaf)

shoulder

sticks

gorge

rivet

FOLDING FAN

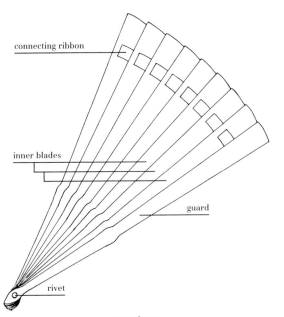

connecting ribbon

inner blades

guard

rivet

BRISÉ FAN

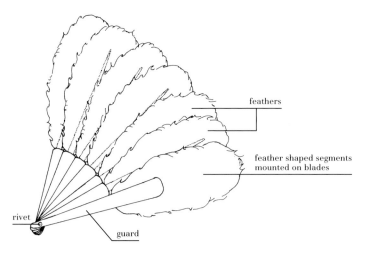

feathers

feather shaped segments
mounted on blades

rivet

guard

FEATHER (OR FEATHER-SHAPED) BRISÉ FAN

258

APPENDIX II

·························

Fan Types and Glossary

The vocabulary developed in one specialty may be misleading if not meaningless to those working in another field. This poses a problem in the case of interdisciplinary objects such as fans, which span many different materials and media. Clearly, one cannot hope for an art Esperanto; but a simplified terminology could encourage fruitful exchange as interdependence grows between the various branches of the arts and the scientific research that supports them.

Words frequently encountered in fan context are listed below, not all of which appear in the text. Those judged misleading or local in application were given quotation marks and synonyms. Others were passed over as too restrictive or inclusive. The catalogue's pared-down vocabulary represents a modest attempt at simplification. Every change exacts its price. In this case, it is the loss of some color and convenience.

A l'Anglaise. (Fr. = "English style") Having a single leaf glued directly to its supporting ribs, which are exposed on the reverse.

Applied Figures Fan. A colorful type of China export fan distinguished by court scenes with many figures, each having an applied painted ivory face and an applied silk garment with design to scale. The traditional names – "Mandarin," "Hundred Faces," and "Thousand Faces" – are less informative than the one suggested.[1]

Articulated Fan. A fan with a moving part or parts, usually enclosed in an oval medallion and activated by a slender rod located beneath or alongside it.

Blades. The sticks of a brisé fan. *See* Brisé.

Brisé. (Fr. = "broken") A leafless fan composed of overlapping blades, usually of equal length, held by a rivet at the base and connected by a ribbon at or near the upper edge. *See* Brisé, feather; Brisé, feather-shaped; Ribbon.

Brisé, Circular. Similar in shape to, but distinct from, the cockade. *See* Cockade.

Brisé, Feather. A variant brisé type in which the upper section of the blades is composed of feathers, held together by an invisible string.

Brisé, Feather-shaped. Similar to the feather brisé, but with textile segments shaped like feathers replacing the real article.

Broken Fan. Composed of separately ribboned sections, which fall apart when the fan is opened in the wrong direction (*right to left*) and which can be visually reintegrated by reopening in the normal way (*left to right*), causing the sections to re-engage.

Cabriolet. A folding fan with two or even three leaves mounted concentrically so that a portion of the widely spaced sticks is visible between the leaves.

Camaïeu. A fan painted entirely in shades of one color is described as *en camaïeu. See* Grisaille.

Cartouche. An ornamental frame enclosing a small scene, monogram, or other design element. *See* Medallion; Reserve; Vignette.

Celluloid. The brand-name for a manmade material used between 1860 and the 1950s, made of nitrated cellulose fibers mixed with camphor and other plasticizers, subjected to heat and pressure before being machined, molded, or pressed. It could be tinted any color to imitate tortoiseshell, ivory, or horn.

"Chassepot". A synonym for "Articulated" (q.v.).

"Chicken Skin". The old name for "fine vellum" or uterine parchment. *See* Skin.

Chinoiserie. (1) A European decorative style using oriental motifs or (2) European objects produced in that style, as distinct from Chinese objects made for export.

Cockade. (Fr. *cocarde*, a ribbon rosette worn on the hat as a badge of patriotism) A fan with a pleated leaf opening 360° around the upper end of its long handle or handles. Some examples can be retracted into an open-ended case/handle.

Découpé Fan. (Fr. *découpé* = "cutout") A fan with a leaf of skin, paper, or textile, cut out or stamped out in a decorative pattern.

Domino. A wooden block for printing paper sheets about 30.5 cm. x 41 cm. (12 in. x 16 in.) used for inexpensive wallpaper, chest lining, and fan leaves. The *dominotier* was the maker of these papers, and fans resembling them are described as in the *dominotier* style.

Domino Fan. A fan with view holes cut in the leaf. The mask fan is a variant of this type. The word *domino* in other contexts can mean a mask or an enveloping cape, hence its application to a fan that can conceal identity.

Expanding Fan. A fan with a movable leaf not glued to its supporting frame and capable of being slipped down, in a closed position, to shorten the height by half or slipped upward on its ribs to restore the normal size. *See* Folding Fan (2).

Folding Fan. (1) A fan with a continuous pleated leaf supported by sticks and folding together between its guards when not in use. The leaf can be single (*see* à l'anglaise) or double, in which case the sticks were inserted by the fan-maker between the two glued thicknesses of the leaf. (2) A fan hinged at the shoulder so that it can fold to fit into a purse or pocket. Invented in the nineteenth century by August Buinot, who called it a "pocket fan."

Gouache. An opaque watercolor medium using pigments mixed with water, gum, honey, or other thickener.

Grisaille. Painting in shades of gray, using only black and white. Fans in grisaille were considered appropriate for mourners.

Guard(s). The outermost sticks, usually heavier and more decorated than the inner sticks, which they protect.

Handscreen. *See* Rigid.

"Head." A term favored by English writers to designate the base or rivet end of the fan. Possibly a confusing term for what is, in the position of use, the fan's lower end.

Horn. A natural plastic obtained from horns, hooves, and nails of various animals, rendered malleable with heat, then pressed or cast. *See* Reformed protein.

Hornbeam. A wood that was plentiful in the Massachusetts South Shore area in the late nineteenth century. It was especially suited for fan sticks as it did not warp, took a high polish, and lent itself to artistic "graining."

Houlette. A traditional pastoral attribute consisting of a shepherd's staff ending in a small shovel to pick up clods of earth and direct them at straying sheep. Another instrument of ovine crowd control was the crook, with a bent end to fit around the sheep's neck or leg for individual retrieval. Both types appear in fans with the popular pastoral theme.[2]

Japanning. A process developed in Europe to create a substitute for the unobtainable Oriental lacquer, using varnish, a shellac mixture, and spirits of wine. The resulting shiny surface dried by evaporation. *See* Shellac.

"Jenny Lind". A term of limited usage designating the feather-shaped brisé fan associated with the singer's American debut. *See* Brisé, feather- shaped.

Lacquer. A medium in which resin, made soluble by certain additives, is applied in multiple coats to give objects a hard and lustrous finish. The true lacquer of China and Japan is based on resin from *Rhus vernicifera*, a variety of sumac known in eighteenth-century Europe as the Tsi, Ci, or Chiaram tree. Each coat applied had to dry very slowly in a moist atmosphere, by oxidation. The *Rhus vernicifera* does not grow in Europe, hence the need to develop substitutes.[3]

Leaf. The pleated band of a folding fan, carrying the principal decoration.

Leaf, Divided. *See* Cabriolet.

Leaf, Pierced. *See* Découpé; Domino.

Lorgnette. A fan with a magnifying lens set into the guard stick or the rivet.

"Mandarin". *See* Applied Figures Fan.

Medallion. A framed oval or round, usually enclosing a portrait or monogram.

Minuet. (Possibly from Fr. = "small") A diminutive brisé fan, especially one of horn, popular between 1810 and 1830. The term evokes an inappropriate image, since the heyday of the minuet dance was the second half of the eighteenth century.

Mother-of-Pearl (nacre). The iridescent lining of a group of shells from pearl-producing mollusks, especially the great pearl oyster, *Meleagrina margaritifera.* The mantle surrounding the animal lays down the lustrous mineral lining in parallel folds, causing the iridescence. The golden-lip variety comes from the Philippines, the black-lip from Tahiti and Cook Islands, and a white type from Australia.

Mount. Used by some to designate the leaf. Possibly a confusing term, since *la monture* means "the sticks" in French and Webster defines the mount as "the frame, support."

"Neapolitan Shell". A dealers' term for the pressed or cast imitation shell common in nineteenth- and twentieth-century sticks. The source was usually horn, but celluloid was also used, and can be identified by laboratory testing. Where markings resembling those of tortoiseshell show the intention of the maker, the material is called "faux tortoiseshell." When the material is unmarked, the animal source unknown, and the processing problematical, the term "reformed protein" reflects those uncertainties. *See* Reformed Protein.[4]

"Pagoda Sticks". Unaccountably dubbed "Pagoda" by Rhead (1910) and followers, the sticks appear more classic in inspiration, resembling the *fasces* borne by ancient Roman lictors as symbols of authority. The slim columns also suggest the legs of a "Gothic" chair designed by Charles Manwaring in 1760, as pointed out in *Fans from*

the East (p. 52 and notes 15, 16). *Colonnette sticks* might be a more useful name for them. (See 1976.323.)

Palisander. A rosewood popular in eighteenth-century France for furniture and the decorative arts.

Parasolette. A cockade fan resembling a miniature parasol, capable of angle adjustment.

Parchment. An animal skin prepared as a surface for writing or artwork. In fan literature, the word usually has been understood as referring to the prepared skin of a sheep, but the dictionary definition is "the skin of a lamb, sheep, goat, young calf, or other animal, prepared for writing on." Reed notes that contrary to the popular belief that it is easy to sort out the goats from the sheep, it is extremely difficult to distinguish between the parchment made from their skins.[5] Since the animal source is problematic, but its protein presence can be determined scientifically, the words "parchment" and "vellum" have been replaced in this text by *skin. See* Vellum.

Piqué. (Fr. = "pricked, dotted") A form of inlaid decoration, usually silver, gold, or steel dots, set into tortoiseshell, ivory, horn, or mother-of-pearl. Invented by the seventeenth-century Neapolitan Laurentini, the process includes both *cloué* ("nailed") and *posé* ("laid") work.[6]

Reformed Protein. Although horn was the most obvious source for imitation tortoiseshell, related proteinaceous material such as hooves was certainly used. Made soft and pliable by boiling, heat, and pressure, the protein material could be reformed by pressing or casting, and could be tinted and given a high polish. See cat. no. 89.

Reserve. A plain area left in a decorated surface to allow for a different type of design, e.g., a miniature landscape, a monogram, or a portrait. *See* Cartouche; Vignette; Medallion.

Ribbon. The connecting ribbon of a brisé fan is usually discontinuous, being made up of separate segments glued to the right half of each obverse blade and the right side of each reverse, thus controlling the exact degree to which the blade can move in either direction.

Ribs. The upper portion of the sticks of a folding fan is often made of a different material from the lower portion. They support the leaf. They are "slips" to many English writers and *brins* to the French. *See* Shoulder.

Rigid. A fixed fan that does not fold, such as the handscreen, is known as a rigid fan. It is often decorated with feathers.

Rivet. The metal pin holding the sticks or the blades together at their base. Originally it passed through a hole in each stick and was flattened on the outside over the ivory or mother-of-pearl washers. Removal for repair was difficult until the introduction of a two-part rivet with a hollow, threaded tube and a screw fitting into it, which was easy to remove. A paste jewel often finished the screw end.[7]

Shellac. (From Sanskrit *lac* = "100,000," referring to the number of shell lice) In India the exudation of shell lice and their host trees produced a gum or resin, which could be distilled to make stick lac or purified seed lac, an item of trade with Turks, Arabs, and Persians long before European interest awakened. By the sixteenth century it had traveled from the Near East to Venice and thence to the rest of Europe. Early japanning with shellac was done in England, which exported finished articles back to Venice. It was Europe's substitute for the Oriental lacquer, which was unobtainable. Most of the European objects commonly described as "lacquered" are actually *japanned.*

Shoulder. The widening of the guard sticks just below the leaf's lower edge, marking the point at which ribs meet the lower sticks, and possibly strengthening this point of weakness. On many sticks made in the 1740s, the shoulder is not well defined. It was most prominent in fans of the first half of the eighteenth century and in the mid-nineteenth.

Skin. The term used to designate a leaf from an animal source without attempting to identify the specific species or to make a quality judgment about the product. It includes the traditional names "parchment," "vellum," and "chicken skin" (uterine parchment).

Sticks. The framework or skeleton of the folding fan, consisting of the outer sticks or guards and the thinner inner sticks (in French, the *panaches* and the *brins*, respectively). For clarity, the sticks of the brisé fan are called "blades" in this text.

Thumbguard. A short section of tortoiseshell, ivory, or bone inlaid near the rivet on the right (*obverse*) guard to protect it from wear.

Tortoiseshell. The shell of the tortoise, or land turtle, was rarely used for luxury objects. Instead, they were fashioned of plates from the carapaces of three species of marine turtles: the delicious green turtle (*Chelonia mydas*), the loggerhead (*Caretta caretta*) and, especially, the hawksbill (*Eretmochelys imbricata*), which alone was blessed (or cursed) with the beautiful mottled shell of amber, brown, and red, and blond plates on its belly. The plates of the green turtle are dull pale brown, those of the loggerhead a rich chestnut.

Tortoiseshell, Blond. The blond plates from the belly of the hawksbill were imitated by pale yellow or amber sticks of reformed protein (q.v.).

Tortoiseshell, Faux. The markings imitating tortoiseshell were produced by staining the "shell" with various chemicals, discussed in the introductory essay, "The Almost Incredible Commerce."

Varnish. A mixture of spirits, gum lac, and siccative (drying) agents. In contrast to the true lacquer of the Orient, European varnish dried by evaporation. Varnish was the medium of the japanning process.

"Vellum". In fan literature, the term "vellum" has had quality overtones and has been understood as a high-grade parchment, specifically from calfskin. The etymology supports this (Mid. Eng. *veel* = "calf"), but the dictionary defines it as "a fine-grained unsplit lambskin, kidskin, or calfskin especially prepared for writing on or for binding books." [8] Preparatory steps included a dehairing bath, scraping, stretching, and drying on a frame. As a result of this process, the fibers were rearranged so that the skin could be divided into layers. The dehairing bath was, ideally, low in tannin, for the presence of tannin in quantity would result in leather. Since the animal source is undetermined and the exact process (amount of tannin, for example) unknown, the word "vellum" is replaced in this text by "skin" with regret, since it is a word of rich associations.

"Vernis Martin". The varnish named for the four famous Martin brothers, active in the mid-eighteenth century, was probably based on copal. At one time, any superior piece of lacquerwork or japanned work was attributed to the celebrated Martins, but little can be authenticated: nothing was signed and they are not known to have worked on fans at all. "Vernis Martin" fans in the old terminology usually meant japanned fans from the first quarter of the century, i.e., before the Martin period. Much good work had been done before them, especially at the Ouvrages de la Chine at the Gobelins, under the leadership of Gérard Dagly, from Liége via Berlin (1713). Dagly's varnish was called *vernis de Gobelins*.[9]

Vignette. A picture that shades off gradually into its surrounding ground, without the decorative frame of a cartouche or the formal border of the medallion.

l. Julia Hutt, "Chinese Fans and Fans from China," *Fans from the East* (London, 1978), p. 33, suggests "Applied Figure" as the appropriate term.

2. See M. L. Ryder, *Sheep and Man* (London, 1983), p. 663: Spenser's *The Shepherd's Calendar* for December shows a staff with a crook on one end and a *houlette* on the other.

3. See Hans Huth, *Lacquer in the West: The History of a Craft and an Industry, 1550-1950* (Chicago, 1971).

4. The "Neapolitan" part of the name recalls the fact that the tortoiseshell industry was already established in Naples by the late fifteenth century. See Carson I. A. Ritchie, *Shell Carving: History and Technique* (South Brunswick and New York, 1974), pp. 162-92.

5. Ronald Reed, *Ancient Skins, Parchments and Leathers* (London and New York, 1972), p. 44.

6. Holes were made with the bow drill in ivory and started in tortoiseshell softened by heat or boiling water. Small gold or silver nails were forced into the shell while still soft to become permanently fixed as the shell cooled.

7. See Nancy Armstrong, *A Collector's History of Fans* (London, 1974), pp. 52-54.

8. See Reed, *Ancient Skins, Parchments and Leathers*, p. 127. "Thus nowadays the word vellum does not necessarily imply the use of calf skin, merely parchment from *any* animal which is both thin and strong."

9. See Armstrong, *The Book of Fans* (Surrey, 1978), pp. 58-67, and Henri Havard, *Dictionnaire de l'ameublement*, 4 vols. (Paris, 1887-90), 4:1651.

SELECTED BIBLIOGRAPHY

Alexander, Hélène. *Fans.* London, 1984.

d'Allemagne, H. R. *Les Accessoires du costume et du mobilier.* Paris, 1928.

Armstrong, Nancy. *A Collector's History of Fans.* London, 1974.

——. *The Book of Fans.* New Malden, Surrey, 1978.

——. *Fans* . London, 1984.

——. *Fans from the Fitzwilliam.* Cambridge, England, 1985.

Bennett, Anna, with Ruth Berson. *Fans in Fashion.* San Francisco, 1981.

Blondel, Spire. *Histoire des éventails chez tous les peuples et à toutes époques.* Paris, 1875.

Boehn, Max von. *Modes and Manners.* Translated by Joan Joshua. 4 vols. London, 1935.

Commoner, Lucy A. *Folding Fans.* Washington, D.C.: Cooper-Hewitt Museum, 1986.

Coutts, Herbert. *The Indispensible Fan: The Story of the Fan in Society.* Edinburgh: Edinburgh City Art Center, 1984.

Crossman, Carl L. *The China Trade.* Princeton, N.J., 1972.

Cust, Lionel. *Catalogue of the Collection of Fans and Fan Leaves Presented to the Trustees of the British Museum by the Lady Charlotte Schreiber.* London, 1893.

Davenport, Millia. *The Book of Costume.* 2 vols. New York, 1948.

DeJong, M. C. *Waaiers & Mode 18e eeuw tot heden.* The Hague: Dutch Costume Museum, c. 1980.

Dorrington-Ward, Carol, editor. *Fans from the East.* New York, 1978.

Eitner, Lorenz E. A. *The Flabellum of Tournus.* College Art Association of America, sponsored by the Archeological Institute of America, 1941.

Fan Circle. *Bulletin of the Fan Circle of America.* (1975-).

Fan Guild of Boston. *Fan Leaves.* Boston, 1961.

Flory, M. A. *A Book About Fans: A History of Fans and Fan-painting.* New York, 1895.

Gostelow, Mary. *The Fan.* Dublin, 1976.

Green, Bertha de Vere. *A Collector's Guide to Fans Over the Ages.* London, 1975.

Grimal, Pierre. *Dictionnaire de la mythologie grécque et romaine.* Paris, 1969.

Havard, Henri. *Dictionnaire de l'ameublement et de la décoration depuis le XIIIe sicle jusqua' à nos jours.* 4 vols. Paris, 1887-90.

Hind, Arthur M. *Giovanni Battista Piranesi: A Critical Study.* London, 1922.

Hunter, Dard. *Papermaking: The History and Technique of an Ancient Craft.* New York, 1974.

Huth, Hans. *Lacquer in the West: The History of a Craft and an Industry, 1550-1950.* Chicago, 1971.

Kopplin, Monika. *Kompositionen im Halbrund.* Stuttgart-Zurich, 1984.

Lami, E.-O. *Dictionnaire encyclopédique et biographique de l'industrie et des arts industriels.* Vol. 4. Paris, 1884.

Levey, Santina M. *Lace: A History.* London: Victoria and Albert Museum, 1983.

Mayer, Carol E. *Fans.* Vancouver, B. C.: Vancouver Museum, 1983.

Mayor, Susan. *Collecting Fans.* New York, 1980.

Musée de la Mode et du Costume. *L'Eventail: Miroir de la belle époque.* Intro. by Madeleine Delpierre. Paris, 1985.

Oldham, Esther. "American Victorian Fans: 'Allen Fans,'" Part 1. *The Antiques Journal* (August 1953): pp. 20-22.

——. "American Victorian Fans: 'Allen Fans,'" Part 2. *The Antiques Journal* (September 1953): pp. 20-22.

——. "Fans of the Paper Stainers: Dominotier and Imagier," Part 1. *Hobbies* (December 1959): pp. 28-29.

——. "Fans of the Paper Stainers: Dominotier and Imagier," Part 2. *Hobbies* (January 1960): pp. 28-30.

——. "Hand- or Fire-Screens: Their Use and Ornament." *The Connoisseur Year Book*, 1961: pp. 94-100.

——. "America's First Fan Factory," Part 1. *Spinning Wheel* (January-February 1972): pp. 62-64.

——. "America's First Fan Factory," Part 2. *Spinning Wheel* (March 1972), pp. 8-10.

Percival, MacIver. *The Fan Book*. London, 1920.

Pigler, Andres. *Barockthemen, eine auswahl von verzeighnissen zur ikonographie des 17. und 18. jahrhunderts*. Budapest, 1965.

Powys, Marian. *Lace and Lace-making*. Boston, 1953.

Redgrave, Samuel. Preface to South Kensington, *Catalogue of the Loan Exhibition of Fans*. London, 1870.

Reed, Ronald. *Ancient Skins, Parchments and Leathers*. London and New York, 1972.

Rhead, George Woolliscroft. *History of the Fan*. Philadelphia, 1910.

Ritchie, Carson I. A. *Shell Carving: History and Technique*. South Brunswick and New York, 1974.

Rosenberg, Marc. *Alte und Neue Facher aus der Wettbewerbung und Austellung zu Karlsruhe*. Vienna, 1891.

Salwey, C. M. *Fans of Japan*. London, 1894.

Savary des Bruslons, Jacques. *Dictionnaire universel de commerce, d'histoire et des arts et métiers*. Edited by Philemon-Louis Savary. 5 vols. Copenhagen, 1760.

Schreiber, Lady Charlotte. *Fans and Fan Leaves*. English: London, 1888, Foreign: London, 1890.

Stalker, John, and George Parker. *A Treatise of Japanning and Varnishing, 1688*. Introduction by H. D. Molesworth. Levittown, N. Y., 1972.

Standen, Edith A. "Instruments for Agitating the Air." *Metropolitan Museum of Art Bulletin* 23, no. 7 (March 1965): pp. 243-257.

Tal, Felix. *De Waaier: Collectie Felix Tal*. Utrecht, 1967.

Uzanne, Octave. *The Fan*. London, 1884.

INDEX